The Economics of Hydroelectric Power

NEW HORIZONS IN ENVIRONMENTAL ECONOMICS

Series Editors: Wallace E. Oates, *Professor of Economics, University of Maryland, USA* and Henk Folmer, *Professor of General Economics, Wageningen University and Professor of Environmental Economics, Tilburg University, The Netherlands*

This important series is designed to make a significant contribution to the development of the principles and practices of environmental economics. It includes both theoretical and empirical work. International in scope, it addresses issues of current and future concern in both East and West and in developed and developing countries.

The main purpose of the series is to create a forum for the publication of high quality work and to show how economic analysis can make a contribution to understanding and resolving the environmental problems confronting the world in the twenty-first century.

Recent titles in the series include:

The Economics of Hydroelectric Power

Brian K. Edwards, PhD
Brian K. Edwards Associates

NEW HORIZONS IN ENVIRONMENTAL ECONOMICS

Edward Elgar
Cheltenham, UK · Northampton, MA, USA

Published by
Edward Elgar Publishing Limited
Glensanda House
Montpellier Parade
Cheltenham
Glos GL50 1UA
UK

Edward Elgar Publishing, Inc.
136 West Street
Suite 202
Northampton
Massachusetts 01060
USA

A catalogue record for this book is available from the British Library

Library of Congress Cataloguing in Publication Data
Edwards, B. K. (Brian Keith), 1954–
    The economics of hydroelectric power / Brian K. Edwards.
      p. cm. — (New horizons in environmental economics)
    Includes bibliographical references and index.
      1. Electric utilities. 2. Hydroelectric power plants—Economic aspects. 3. Dams—Economic aspects. I. Title. II. Series.

    HD9685.A2E36 2003
    333.91'4—dc21

                                                      2003052824

ISBN 1 84064 536 9

Printed and bound in Great Britain by MPG Books Ltd, Bodmin, Cornwall

In Congress, water projects are a kind of currency, like wampum, and water development itself is a kind of religion.

Marc Reisner, *Cadillac Desert*

To

my wife Becca,

my children Martin and Natalie,

and

to George Tolley

Contents

Preface

This book emerges from previous research and work in the area of hydroelectric power. I have long been struck by the lack of any appreciable literature that focused on economic issues relating to the operation, regulation and impacts of dams and hydroelectric power. Much of the research in the area has been confined to the power systems (engineering) literature while, for the most part, economics research has addressed some of the environmental issues associated with water use, including valuing damages to ecosystems and valuing the recreational benefits of water resources. One of the aims of this book is to provide the reader with a relatively self-contained introduction to the economics of dams and hydroelectric power. Given the nature of this subject and given the dearth of previously published books on this subject, it has been difficult to decide on issues of coverage, scope and complexity. I am just as certain that anyone who reads this book will notice that I have excluded some topics altogether, and placed too little emphasis on others, and probably have placed too much emphasis on still other topics. Any reader who has either conducted research or worked in this area will have a particular level of expertise in a topic that they will believe should have been given considerably more emphasis here. In any event, what I have presented no doubt reflects my own vision of how such a subject should be placed in an economics context. Since I cannot possibly cover every topic, I can only hope that this book will provide a foundation upon which the additional topics can be analysed. I would be delighted if this book spurred additional research on many of those areas that receive little or no attention here.

I could easily devote this preface to subjects either downplayed or excluded from treatment altogether, but I will mention a few. I completely ignore issues of uncertainty with respect to reservoir inflows, prices, demand and so on. I also ignore game-theoretic aspects of dams and hydroelectric power. Interested readers are referred to Bushnell's (1998) paper on the competition in the western US electricity market, and Batstone and Scott's (1998) paper that examines the relationship between spot and contract markets in managing hydroelectric power scheduling. I will address some of the environmental issues relating to dam operations, but these will largely be confined to integrating operational restrictions into our analysis of dam operations. In Chapter 7, I will also address recreational issues relating to downstream uses of water, but these will be limited to one recreational activity, namely angling, and will be used as an example illustrating one possible approach to estimating the benefits of the operating restrictions on hydroelectric power operators that we discuss in various chapters. I will not address possible linkages between hydroelectric power generation and water use in irrigated agriculture. The reader is referred to Edwards et al. (1996) for a discussion of how current methods of pricing hydroelectric power in the western United States affect input substitution in irrigated agriculture. Moreover, issues relating to conjunctive water use, that is, jointly managing groundwater and surface water and possibly integrating this analysis into water use for hydroelectric power generation, will also not be addressed. The reader is referred to the pioneering work of Oscar Burt (1964). A recent paper by Hodge (2001) continues the task of integrating dam operations with agricultural and recreational uses, fruitful work that I am certain will continue to develop. I am sure that some very interesting and useful research awaits those who venture into these (and other) areas. Despite these and other omissions and shortcomings, I hope the reader will take from this book a foundation upon which energy, recreational, environmental, agriculture and other issues relating to the use and impacts of dams and hydroelectric power can be better understood, and possibly integrated into more complete analyses of hydroelectric power.

Another body of work has focused on what has become known as adaptive management. This takes a broad multidisciplinary approach to analysing many issues, including those involving managing hydroelectric power generating facilities. This approach has been applied to managing the Glen Canyon dam in Arizona. The interested reader is urged to consult the work by Walters (1986) and to pursue other sources, for an introduction to this subject and examples of its application to a broad array of environmental management issues. An area of modelling that has received considerable recent attention is what has become known as agent-based modelling, which holds the potential for answering many questions about managing complex energy systems and understanding their associated environmental impacts. While this book makes no attempt to use this approach to analyse hydroelectricity generating facilities, those interested are referred to a recent collection of papers edited by Axelrod (1997) for an overview on the subject. His *The Evolution of Cooperation* (1985) is also highly recommended.

I also make no attempt to assess the broader political and budgetary issues associated with dams and hydroelectric power. The quote by Reisner (1993) at the beginning of this book will be self-explanatory to anyone who has paid any attention to the large-scale water and hydroelectric projects that sprinkle the landscape and history of the American West. But I cannot help but draw an analogy between water pricing and hydroelectric power pricing, at least in the United States. The environmental and ecological impacts of cheap water are well documented, as any cursory reading of *Cadillac Desert* will reveal. Likewise, hydroelectric power has historically been priced below prevailing market prices for electrical power from other sources. In both cases, such pricing cannot be rationalised from a resource management perspective, discourages water and energy conservation, and can only persist by the cooperation of successful rent-seeking agricultural and energy interests and a complicit government. Moreover, the below-market rates that government-owned and taxpayer-financed facilities receive for hydroelectric power from utilities (and other buyers), are almost always treated as a benefit of operating these facilities, when they should be treated as a cost instead. During the recent energy debacle in California, the Western Area Power Administration found itself in the unfortunate position of having to purchase power on the spot market at historically high rates, only to turn around and sell this same power to their firm customers at much lower contract rates. What energy management objective could possibly have been achieved by such behaviour under such circumstances is difficult to fathom. But even without these complications, and in normal times, these facilities can receive higher prices for this power but do not. The power is sold below what economists refer to as its opportunity cost. This price difference can then be thought of as a taxpayer-financed subsidy to purchasers of this hydroelectric power. Moreover, to the extent that the current pricing of hydroelectric power is responsible for additional fluctuations in downstream flows, an issue that we will indeed address later on, any environmental or ecological damages attributable to these additional fluctuations might be considered, at the very least, damages that are partly taxpayer-financed.

In terms of level of complexity, this book is geared to readers familiar with elementary natural resource economics. In my own view, the easiest way to analyse dams and hydroelectric power is within the context of dynamic natural resource models and this bias is reflected in this book. I present a brief introduction to natural resource economics in Chapter 3, but getting through this chapter will require some knowledge of elementary optimal control theory. Economists desiring to learn the basics of optimal control theory are referred to Clark (1976) and Dasgupta and Heal (1979) for introductions that are presented within the context of natural resource economics. Other treatments not tied to natural resource economics are in Chiang (1992), Takayama (1984), Silberberg (1990) and Arrow and Kurz (1970). The collection of articles in Liu (1980) includes applications of these methods to exhaustible and renewable resources. Of course, these are but a very few of the many places where one can learn the rudiments of optimal control theory. More mathematically sophisticated readers are referred to Pontryagin et al. (1962) and Hadley (1964).

We illustrate the results of some of the models presented in this book with a series of simulations. Some of these have been performed using the solver in Microsoft Excel. I have included fairly explicit descriptions of how to implement these models in Excel in the event that the reader is interested in developing their own simulation models. The inspiration for using Microsoft Excel to solve simpler hydroelectricity generation problems comes from Conrad's (1999) wonderful text on resource economics that offers the reader many examples of using Excel to solve a wide variety of natural resource economics problems. Interested readers are strongly urged to seek that book out. In later chapters, our more complex models will require the use of more sophisticated tools. For these simulations, we use the GAMS (Brooke et al. 1998) modelling and simulation program. I have not included the code for these programs, but, of course, will provide that code (and data) to anyone interested in either replicating my results or developing their own hydroelectric power models using that program.

Let me first express my appreciation to Sam Flaim and Richard Howitt, my co-authors of the *Land Economics* (1999) paper that provided the basis for Chapter 7 of this book. Michael Welsh of Christensen Associates provided recreational use values for the Glen Canyon dam and assisted with interpreting this information. I hope I have it right. Clayton Palmer of the Western Area Power Administration provided an opportunity for me and Sam Flaim to present some of our modelling results during a recent hydroelectric power modelling workshop. Comments by him, Tom Veselka (Argonne National Laboratory) and other participants are appreciated. David Harpman (US Department of the Interior, Bureau of Reclamation) and Lars Nesheim provided comments on the *Land Economics* paper that evolved into Chapter 7. The comments and suggestions of Fred Disheroon (US Department of Justice), who was kind enough to review a draft of the legislative material in Section 2.2, are appreciated. Of course, all of these individuals are absolved of any responsibility for any shortcomings that remain. The folks at Edward Elgar Publishing have been far too patient. So has my wife, Becca.

Let me conclude this preface with the following dialogue from John Steinbeck's *Sweet Thursday*:

> *'I can see it now,' said Mack.*
> *'Ghosts?' Eddie asked.*
> *'Hell no,' said Mack, 'chapters...'*

1.   Introduction

Sometime during the middle 1970s, one of my fellow undergraduate students went on to study for a PhD in economics. She decided on energy economics as her field of specialization. At that time, such a field was virtually non-existent and, from what I recall, such a specialty had to be co-developed by this student and one of her advisors. Interestingly, this was just a few years after the first energy crisis and policy-makers were grappling with how best to deal with the new problems of rising prices in what until then had been treated as steady (and inexpensive) sources of energy supply. Since then, energy economics has become a more important field in economics and courses in energy economics are now offered as undergraduate electives. Despite the growth of energy economics as an elective for undergraduate students, as well as an applied field in many graduate-level economics curricula, very little economics research has been conducted that focuses specifically on dams and hydroelectric power. Most academic articles on hydroelectric power can be found in the various engineering journals and most textbook treatments of hydroelectric power can be found in textbooks devoted to power systems (a specialty in engineering). The few cases where dams and hydroelectric power have been treated in the economics literature consist of articles in the energy and environmental economics literature, and most of these address valuation issues involving recreational activities that are either enhanced or hindered by the existence of dams.

As a result, one of the objectives of this book is to create a somewhat self-contained introduction to the economics of dams and hydroelectric power. Even though hydroelectric power makes up approximately 10 per cent of total electrical generation in the United States, and one-third of all countries depend on hydropower for over one-half of their electricity, a number of energy and environmental issues emerge that justify a separate treatment. Moreover, hydroelectric power generation is but one of many functions of dams. One-third of European dams, for example, are used to generate hydroelectric power, with another 20 per cent being used for irrigation. Nearly two-thirds of Asian dams are for irrigation, with only 7 per cent being used for hydroelectric power generation. In North and Central America, dam use is almost equally divided between irrigation, hydroelectric power, water supply, flood control and recreation. Nearly one-quarter of South American dams are used for hydroelectricity generation. For Africa, one-half of the dams are used for irrigation and another 20 per cent are used for water supply. Finally, nearly one-half of the dams in Austral-Asia are used for water supply while 20 per cent are used for hydroelectric power. The reader is referred to International Commission on Large Dams (1998) and World Commission on Dams (2000) for detailed statistics on the worldwide distribution and use of dams.

These statistics suggest that any analysis of dams or hydroelectric power be given a broader water management backdrop. To this end, one of the objectives of this book is to dispel the notion that hydroelectric power generation represents the principal purpose of dams while the other functions of dams are merely residual. An opposite ordering would bring us far closer to reality. Ultimately, the purpose of dams is to manage water, and hydroelectric generation is but one of the many by-products of dams and just one of the many possible sources of the benefits of dams. The foundation of the dynamic models presented in this book will be an equation of motion for the water resource, and much of the analysis that follows will be driven by the timing of water releases, and how water releases feedback into the equation of motion to determine changes in content, elevation and dam head. Indeed, one of the major concerns over dam use has been the high rate at which water has been withdrawn from lakes, rivers and aquifers. According to the World Commission on Dams (2000), annual water withdrawals for all uses from these sources amount to about 3 800 cubic kilometres which is double the rate of 50 years ago. The world population may stabilize sometime during the middle of the twenty-first century, but increased urbanization and rising economic standards will continue to place additional strains on water supplies.

A second objective of this book is to present, as far as possible, an overview of the existing state of economic analysis of dams and hydroelectricity generating facilities. In this regard, writing this book has become somewhat of an adventure. Much of the literature on hydroelectric power comes from the engineering fields, while virtually all of the economic analysis can be found scattered amongst a few journal articles and as examples in textbooks on cost–benefit analysis and natural resource economics. Another area of the economics literature that deals with dams and hydroelectric power actually addresses many of the environmental issues mentioned above, namely, the literature on non-market valuation. For example, there have been a number of articles that have attempted to estimate the value of recreational activities made possible by the existence of dams. We will refer to this literature where appropriate. A final objective of this book comes from my experience of attempting to write it. Here I refer to the very scattered nature of information on dams and hydroelectric power. I hope that this book will make it easier for future researchers to find information on hydroelectric power and provide a basis from which future research can stem. I also hope that the Bibliography will provide a fairly complete listing of the economic literature on dams and hydroelectric power and point the reader to the most important literature from a variety of fields.

The last few years have seen many changes in the energy industries in the United States and other countries. In the United States, many states have opted to deregulate their energy industries. Deregulation of the energy industry in Britain pre-dates deregulation in the United States by nearly a decade, and was applied to the whole country rather than to individual states on a piecemeal basis (*The Economist*, 2001). The intention of deregulation has been to create workable markets for energy that will improve the efficiency with which energy is produced, transmitted and distributed, and eventually lower energy prices to consumers. As an added benefit, proponents of deregulation hope that the pricing signals will direct energy resources to their most efficient use and provide incentives to users to conserve energy.

However, as any observer of the energy industry realizes, there is much more at stake than economic efficiency. In most cases, energy and air pollution are joint products. When left to markets alone, socially unacceptable levels of air pollution are often the result. Nuclear power, which avoids the air pollution problems associated with traditional fossil fuel use, presents a host of possibly much more serious longer-term waste storage issues. Moreover, the public has been reluctant to accept these facilities based on fears of what could happen in the event of malfunctions. Despite arguments that hydroelectric generation always displaces emissions of pollutants, critics of hydroelectric power cite increased production of greenhouse gases. While we may eventually see the day where more environmentally benign sources of energy replace traditional non-renewable forms of energy, the day when these technologies become cost-effective is likely to be discussed in the future tense for some time.

In contrast, one of the alleged benefits of hydroelectric power is that it produces no direct emissions and does not create the need for controversial high-level waste storage facilities. Also, dams have also not created their own set of 'not-in-my-backyard' (NIMBY) concerns such as have stigmatized nuclear power facilities and proposed nuclear waste storage facilities. Proponents of hydroelectric power cite displacement of fossil-fuel emissions as an added benefit (Francfort, 1997). All else being equal, a megawatt of hydroelectric power generation will produce no direct emissions while a megawatt of fossil-fuel power generation will release emissions that can contribute to ground-level ozone formation or acid rain deposition. Despite these benefits, hydroelectric power generation brings its own set of environmental concerns. Unlike most fossil-fuel energy generating plants, hydroelectric facility construction is virtually irreversible. While some smaller dams have recently been torn down, it is virtually impossible to fathom how the Hoover dam could be decommissioned and taken apart without causing enormous energy and economic disruptions in the American West.

Even the act of building a dam causes dramatic changes to the environment, before any hydroelectric power is generated, and before any of the other water management services provided by the dam are realized. The Xiaolangdi and Three Gorges dams in China are two recent cases in point. Hundreds of thousands of people are already being relocated by their construction, and many cities and towns will be submerged once they are completed. The Yellow River, which will feed the Xiaolangdi dam, has already been stopped. Proponents of this dam point to the need to control flooding which they argue has killed hundreds of thousands of people over the last 50 years (*The Economist*, 1997). Once the Yangzi River has been stopped, it will take nearly ten years to fill the reservoir behind the Three Gorges dam. By then, the number of displaced persons will number nearly 2 million, and cause irreversible damage to archaeological sites. Once completed, the Three Gorges dam will have an installed capacity of 17 680 megawatts, which will make it the second largest dam in the world, behind the

Turukhansk dam in Russia, but place it well ahead of the Itaipu (Brazil/Paraguay), Grand Coulee (USA) and Grui (Venezuela) dams.

Once a dam is completed and in operation, a whole host of new environmental concerns come into play. One of the benefits of hydroelectric power is that power plants can adjust their rate of generation quickly, but this very flexibility leads to one of the principal set of environmental concerns, namely, rapid changes in the downstream flow of rivers. These fluctuating flows can erode downstream sandbanks, change the deposition of downstream river sediment, which can alter the ecological make-up of the downstream environment, and can degrade the quality of downstream recreational activities such as fishing. Interestingly, reducing the degree that water releases fluctuate can cause other environmental problems. The construction of the Glen Canyon dam not only brought the Colorado River under control, but also mitigated the positive effects that the annual spring flooding produced before the dam was ever constructed. This flooding replenished downstream sandbanks subject to erosion by the river during the course of the year. To correct this, the United States Bureau of Reclamation has been experimenting with periodic sustained high releases that mimic the spring flooding that used to occur naturally (Collier et al., 1997).

Critics of hydroelectric power have even challenged the often-touted air emissions benefit of hydroelectric power. They cite water in storage dams that often becomes silted with vegetation that, when it rots, emits carbon dioxide and methane, two greenhouse gases. Accordingly, instead of displacing fossil–fuel emissions, hydroelectric power generation can produce its own greenhouse gas emissions that might offset any fossil–fuel emissions it displaces. Two recent studies of the same hydroelectricity generating facility in Brazil came to different conclusions, estimating that the Tucurui reservoir emitted between 5 and 76 tons of methane per square kilometre and between 2378 and 3808 tons of carbon dioxide annually. To the extent that the higher estimates are closer to reality, burning fossil fuels might have been the more environmentally benign option.

When Lewis and Clark first explored the American north-west in the early years of the nineteenth century, they noted in their journals the abundance of Columbia River salmon. Nowadays, salmon populations are threatened there and populations of other fish species are threatened throughout the world. This has led critics of hydroelectric power to blame it for disrupting the movement of many fish species to their spawning sites. In 2000, this very impact caused more than 1500 fishermen and farmers to occupy the Pak Mun hydroelectric dam in the rural north–east of Thailand. Critics of this dam have cited destruction to local fish stocks and damaged irrigation systems. Protestors demanded nothing less than an opening of the dam's floodgates and its eventual demolition (*The Economist*, 2000b). In 1999, the Edwards dam that had blocked the Kennebec River in Maine for 162 years was bulldozed. Since then, stocks of sturgeon, striped bass, Atlantic salmon and alewives have increased, water quality has improved, and more animals, plants and birds now occupy the river's banks (*The Economist*, 2000c). These positive impacts have not gone unnoticed, as over 40 dams throughout the United States have either been removed, or slated for removal. Dam-removal advocates have recently pointed their attention at the Snake River, a main tributary of the Columbia River, where four dams have virtually stopped the flow of salmon.

Dams can also have unforeseen impacts even when they accomplish their intended purposes. Flood control dams often induce people to live closer to rivers, an impact that can be catastrophic. In 1993, floods in Mississippi overwhelmed the dam system, causing billions of dollars in damages to communities along the river. Presumably, these damages would have been less severe had people chosen to locate further from the river. To the extent that irrigation dams are successful, they can also encourage the wasteful use of water, as evidenced by farmers switching from drip and other water-conserving irrigation methods to more wasteful spray methods of irrigation. To the extent that hydroelectric power is sold at below-market rates, as is done in many parts of the United States, electrical irrigation methods are encouraged, possibly inducing farmers to specialize in more water-intensive crops. What else can account for the high share of American cotton grown in Arizona, or, for that matter, the preponderance of golf courses in the Phoenix area?

While hydroelectric power is generally considered a reliable source of electricity, its availability often depends on the whims of nature (French, 1998). Years of low rainfall in Brazil, a country that depends on hydroelectric power for more than 90 per cent of its electricity needs, led Brazil to recently approve the licensing of more than 20 new gas-fired generating plants and to consider the construction of additional nuclear capacity. In the meantime, Brazil faces the possibility of rolling blackouts to bring electricity consumption in line with generating capacity (Reuters, 2001). Shortages of water in the western United States have caused fissures in the deregulation scheme recently promulgated in the state of California (Harden, 2001). With sufficient water, enough power could have been brought into that state to prevent, or at least forestall, the energy problems they now face or, at the very least, to have postponed the revelation of inherent faults in how they went about deregulating their power industry (Verhovek, 2000).

Still, hydroelectric power is important to many countries, and dams will continue to serve this and many other purposes well into the future. The 'large dam' era in the United States, which saw the construction of the Hoover and Grand Coulee dams, also spurred unprecedented economic development in the western United States, and also provided economic stimulus in the midst of the Great Depression. Interested readers are referred to Reisner (1993) for a fascinating account of the water and hydroelectric projects and the roles they have played in recent American history. Many other countries have viewed dam development as an important stepping-stone to economic growth and development. For some time, the World Bank provided financing for hydroelectric power development in many developing countries (*The Economist*, 2000a). Here lies the trade-off. Dams benefit society by providing a relatively inexpensive source of energy, provide a means for reclaiming and storing water for public consumption and irrigation, provide a means by which the unpredictable flow of rivers can be controlled, and provide recreational opportunities both above and below dams. However, the construction and operation of dams and hydroelectric facilities, regardless of how much electricity is generated, how much water is stored or how many floods are prevented, raises its own set of environmental and other issues. Ultimately, all of these issues must be weighed when decisions on the financing, construction and operation of dams are made.

Chapter 2 of this book will begin with an historical introduction to dams, with an emphasis on dam development in the United States. This chapter will also present an overview of the regulation of hydroelectric power, from the beginning of the twentieth century to the present. I hope that readers from other countries will be patient with, and ultimately forgive, my emphasis on the United States. The optimist in me hopes for a second edition, so any background material on legal and institutional issues involving dams in other countries is always welcome.

Chapter 3 will present an overview of natural resource economics. This chapter will begin with exhaustible resources and will derive some basic results from simple exhaustible resource models. The following section will present a simple model of a renewable resource and present some basic results from this model. This chapter should provide the reader with some background in elementary natural resource economics that will prove useful in later chapters. Of course, those familiar with the basics of natural resource economics can skip this chapter.

Chapter 4 will present a brief introduction to the engineering background of how dams work. This chapter will provide the reader with some background on dam operations and introduce some of the terminology that will be used in later chapters. In this chapter, I will discuss the hydrologic cycle, how water is used to generate hydroelectric power, and how hydroelectric power is integrated into existing electricity transmission and distribution systems. I will also present a simple dynamic model that links the supply of water to hydroelectric power generation. This model will serve as the basis for the economic models presented in the remaining chapters of this book.

Chapter 5 will present a simple dynamic model of a hydroelectric power generating facility. The model that we will develop will most closely resemble the dynamic economic models used to analyse such renewable resources as fish. This model will differ from a traditional exhaustible resource model because the water resource will be subject to additions from above the dam. In any case, we will assume the existence of a dam operator that makes decisions on how much water to release from a dam on an hourly basis, and these decisions will be made over the course of many periods.

An important characteristic of water that is used to generate hydroelectric power is the dual role that water plays. First, releasing water in a given period generates hydroelectric power in that period. Second, and as shall be discussed in Chapter 5, the amount of power generation that can occur as water is released will depend on how much water is currently stored behind the dam. This suggests that the water will have two values, a current value resulting from the flow of water through the turbines that generate the hydroelectric power, and a future value resulting from the contribution that the stored water makes to the rate at which releasing water generates hydroelectric power. While this distinction is presented in Chapter 4, we will develop the dual roles of water more formally in Chapter 5.

An important aspect of hydroelectricity generation in the United States is the (for lack of a better phrase) environmental restrictions that limit the flexibility with which water can be released. These restrictions include constraints that require minimum hourly release rates and on how much water release rates can change over time. The first version of this model (presented in Chapter 5) does not include these restrictions. Chapter 6 will integrate these restrictions into the basic model of hydroelectric power generation. We will then examine how these constraints affect the hourly operations of the dam.

Chapter 7 will follow with a case-study involving one of the dams operated by one of the Power Marketing Administrations (PMAs) in the United States, namely, the Glen Canyon dam located on the Colorado River in Arizona. A brief description of this dam will be followed by an adaptation of the model presented in Chapter 6 to it. Much of the analysis presented in this chapter is from an article that appeared in *Land Economics*, co-authored by Richard E. Howitt, Silvio J. Flaim and myself (Edwards et al., 1999). This article addressed how the hourly pricing of hydroelectric power, along with the environmental restrictions imposed on the dam, affect hourly releases of water over the course of a month.

The models presented in Chapters 4 to 7 are of dams that operate independently of one another. However, many dams are connected by a common river and are operated jointly. For these hydraulically-coupled dams, releases from the upstream dam provide water for future release, and subsequent hydroelectric power generation, by the downstream dam. Flows of water through the Columbia River, for example, are controlled by a series of 11 dams. Managing water flows through the Columbia River involves managing all 11 dams simultaneously. In Tasmania, the Derwent Catchment is made up of 16 dams, 10 power stations and a large number of smaller dams. Other such systems can be found in many other countries. Chapter 8 presents a dynamic model of such dam systems and follows the general structure of Chapters 5 and 6. A simple model is presented without environmental or other institutional operating restrictions, and then we examine what happens as a series of environmental constraints are added.

Analogous to Chapter 7, Chapter 9 follows with a case study of the Aspinall Unit, which is made up of three hydraulically-coupled dams: the Blue Mesa, Morrow Point and Crystal dams. This unit is located in south-west Colorado and is operated by the Western Area Power Administration (US Department of Energy) .

Chapter 10 will summarize the major findings of this book and offer suggestions for future research.

2. The uses of dams and hydroelectric power

For how long have people attempted to systematically control the supply and use of water? When was water first used to generate hydroelectric power? How did dams contribute to the economic growth of the United States and other countries? Do dams serve functions other than hydroelectric power generation and do these functions differ between countries? The answers to these and other questions are the subject of this chapter. After presenting a brief history of the development of hydroelectric power, we summarize dam regulation and use with a particular focus on the United States. We also present some statistics on the distribution of dams across the world and how dams are used in different parts of the world.

2.1 A BRIEF HISTORY OF DAMS AND HYDROELECTRIC POWER

Water has been harnessed for irrigation and water supply for many thousands of years. Ruins of irrigation canals over 8000 years old can be found in Mesopotamia and the remains of water dams that date back to at least 3000 BC can be found in Jordan, Egypt and other parts of the Middle East. By about 2000 years ago, the use of dams for irrigation and water supply had spread to the Mediterranean, China and Meso-America. In Sri Lanka and Israel, the remains of embankment dams used to divert water to reservoirs can be found to this day and dams and aqueducts built by Romans still operate. Even the use of water for mechanical purposes is over 2000 years old, when Greeks used flowing water to turn water wheels that ground wheat into flour.

Even though mechanical hydropower was used extensively for milling and pumping by the 1700s, it was not until the late nineteenth century that water was used to generate electricity. In 1880, the Grand Rapids Electric Light and Power Company of Michigan lit 16 brush-arc lamps with a water turbine. The use of hydroelectric power to light city street lamps in Niagara Falls would soon follow. In Canada, 1881 saw a waterwheel plant built at Chaudière Falls by Ottawa Electric Light Company that supplied power for street lighting and local mills. By 1886, approximately 45 water-powered electric plants existed in the United States and Canada and 1900 saw the first international transmission line between Canada and the United States. Hydroelectric power grew so rapidly that it accounted for 15 per cent of electric generating capacity in the United States by 1907. By 1920, hydroelectric power accounted for over 97 per cent of the electricity produced in Canada. In the United States, hydroelectric power accounted for approximately one-third of electric generating capacity by 1940. The American West and Pacific north–west relied on hydroelectric power even more, so that approximately 75 per cent of their electric generating capacity was provided by hydroelectric power (US Department of the Interior, Bureau of Reclamation, 2001b).

The subsequent growth of fossil, nuclear and other power generation has reduced the nation's reliance on hydroelectric power to its current share of 10 per cent. However, certain regions of the United States still rely on hydroelectric power for significant portions of their energy portfolio and inexpensive hydroelectric power fuels much of the irrigated agriculture of the American West. Moreover, many states use hydroelectric power as a supplement to other sources of electricity, a factor that has compounded recent energy problems in California and other western states. Despite increased restrictions on the operations of dams and recent moves to decommission some existing hydroelectricity generating facilities, hydroelectric power will continue to account for a significant share of energy production in the United States.

2.2   DEVELOPMENT AND REGULATION OF HYDROELECTRIC POWER IN THE UNITED STATES

While the development and regulation of hydroelectric power has a long history of federal oversight, the demand and supply of such power has largely been regulated at the state and local level. Unless a dam has been constructed specifically for such federal purposes as flood control or navigation, hydroelectric power generation has to comply with state proprietary water laws. Under the Federal Pollution Control Act, as amended by the Clean Water Act Amendments of 1977 (Clean Water Act), unless state and local environmental laws conflict with federal law, hydroelectric projects must also comply with state and local environmental laws (Disheroon, 1993).

In the beginning of the twentieth century, most hydroelectric power development was private, developed primarily through holding companies so that by 1916, most of the 87 hydroelectric projects in the United States were in private hands. During this period, the federal government increased its role in hydroelectric power development primarily through federal reclamation projects by the United States Bureau of Reclamation (BOR) and water resource projects by the United States Army Corps of Engineers (Corps). Over the years, the Corps has been the largest single producer of hydroelectric power in the United States, and currently operates 75 dams with an installed capacity of over 21 000 megawatts (Disheroon, 1993).

The BOR was created by the Reclamation Act of 1902. This act authorized the Secretary of the Interior to develop irrigation and hydropower projects in 17 western states. The increased involvement by the Bureau of Reclamation was a natural consequence of the need to manage scarce water supplies in the western United States. Despite much of the emphasis on hydroelectric power generation, the development of dams resulted from the need to effectively manage water supplies in a predominantly arid region. Moreover, hydroelectric power was often used during the construction phases of these projects to provide electrical power for the processing of materials, the running of sawmills, concrete plants and construction equipment, and allowed for operation of construction activities during the night. After construction was finished, hydroelectricity was used to power drainage pumps that moved water to higher elevations than was possible with gravity-flow canals. As many of these hydroelectric power facilities found that they had surplus power, it was necessary to establish the terms under which such surplus power could be sold. To that end, the Towns Sites and Development Act (1906) gave the Secretary of the Interior authority to lease surplus power or power privileges (US Department of the Interior, Bureau of Reclamation, 2001b). As a result, surplus power was sold to existing power distribution systems that benefited local industries, towns and the farming community.

Indeed, the Bureau of Reclamation's first hydroelectric facility was constructed to support construction of the Theodore Roosevelt dam, located on the Salt River north-west of Phoenix, Arizona. While the primary purpose of the hydroelectric power was to power construction equipment, the surplus power generated by this plant was sold to the local community (US Department of the Interior, Bureau of Reclamation, 2001b). Public support for additional power led to an expansion of the capacity of this dam, so that in 1909 five generators were placed in operation that provided power for irrigated agriculture and the Phoenix area. This expansion of hydroelectric power encouraged the economic growth of the Phoenix area, including expanding electrically irrigated agriculture to cover more than 10 000 acres, and providing all of the residential and commercial power requirements of the area.

In 1920, the Federal Power Act established the Federal Power Commission, giving them authority to issue licences for developing hydroelectric projects in public lands and on navigable waters. In 1928, the Boulder Canyon Project Act authorized construction of the Hoover dam. Even though initiated before the New Deal, the construction of the Hoover dam has come to symbolize many of the large-scale public works projects that came to characterize the New Deal. Until the 1930s, the Federal Power Commission took a fairly laissez-faire approach to requests for licences for power projects, granting most of these requests with little federal review or oversight. It was not until the administration of President Franklin D. Roosevelt that the role that the federal government currently plays would be established (Disheroon, 1993). The Public Utility Act of 1935 expanded the FPC's jurisdiction, which hitherto had been limited to licensing hydroelectric generation, to include setting wholesale electricity rates. Under this Act, however, regulation of consumer rates remained with state public utility commissions. The administration of Franklin D. Roosevelt also ushered in the 'big dam' period which, in addition to the Hoover dam, saw the construction of many other large multipurpose hydroelectric projects including the Grand Coulee dam on the Columbia River in Washington state (authorized by the Rivers and Harbors Act of 1935) and the Central Valley Project in California. The Tennessee Valley Authority (TVA) was created in 1933 and the Bonneville Project Act of 1937 created the Bonneville Power Administration (BPA). The construction of these dams had much to do with the migration to the west that occurred during the 1930s. During the Second World War, cheap hydroelectric power encouraged firms involved in the defence effort to locate in the west.

From these legal developments, two federal policies emerged: (1) primary federal regulation of the construction and use of private hydroelectric projects; and (2) federal construction and control of the largest such projects. With the exception of increased use of federal subsidies and tax incentives designed to encourage small hydroelectric power development at both existing and new facilities, these two policies remain in effect (Disheroon, 1993).

Even then, the environmental impacts of hydroelectric power generation, including the lowering of water tables brought on by the rapid growth of irrigated agriculture, began to be recognized and would eventually lead to legislation that addressed these environmental impacts. Most of the early legislation laid the groundwork for the construction and operation of hydroelectricity projects, but it would not be until 1968, with the passage of the Wild and Scenic Rivers Act, that these environmental concerns would begin to be addressed. That Act protected rivers in their natural state by excluding them from consideration as hydroelectric power generation sites. One year later, the National Environmental Policy Act (NEPA) required federal agencies to take into account environmental considerations in the construction and operation of hydroelectricity generating facilities. In 1973, the Endangered Species Act listed endangered species and their critical habitat, many of which are directly affected by the construction and operation of dams. In 1946, the Fish and Wildlife Coordination Act was amended to ensure that fish and wildlife would receive equal consideration for protection by federal agencies. Sections 401 and 404 of the Clean Water Act ensured federal and non-federal entities comply with state water quality standards by requiring state certification as a condition to Federal Energy Regulatory Commission (FERC) license approval (Disheroon, 1993).

Other regulations addressed the financing and administration of dams. The Federal Water Power Act of 1920 regulated hydroelectric development of navigable waterways. The Reclamation Project Act of 1939 extended the contract term to 40 years for sale of power or lease of power privileges, giving preference to public entities. The Flood Control Act of 1944 gave the Secretary of the Interior authority to market power from Army Corps of Engineers projects and authorized the Pick-Sloan Missouri Basin Program. The Federal Columbia River Transmission Act of 1974 authorized the Bonneville Power Administration to issue revenue bonds (US Department of the Interior, Bureau of Reclamation, 2001b).

In 1977, the United States Department of Energy was created by the Department of Energy Organization Act. This Act transferred the existing Power Marketing Administrations to the newly created Department of Energy and created the Western Area Power Administration. The Public Utility Regulatory Policies Act (PURPA) of 1978 encouraged small-scale power production facilities; exempted certain hydroelectric projects from federal licensing requirements and required utilities to purchase – at 'avoided cost' rates – power from small production facilities that use renewable resources (US Department of the Interior, Bureau of Reclamation, 2001b).

2.3   WORLDWIDE DAM CONSTRUCTION AND OPERATIONS

Throughout most of the twentieth century, most dam construction occurred in the United States and Europe. However, during the 1960s, dam construction in Asia exceeded European construction, and by the early 1990s Asian dam construction exceeded that in the United States. According to the World Commission on Dams, around 22 000 large dams, close to one-half of the world's large dams, have been built in China, with the vast majority of these built after 1949. The United States currently has over 6390 large dams, India has over 4000 large dams, while Japan has 1200 and Spain has 1000 large dams. Table 2.1 summarizes the regional distribution of dams.

Table 2.1 Distribution of large dams by region

Regions and countries	Number of dams	% of region total	% of world total
Asia	31 340	100.0	65.8
China	22 000	70.2	46.2
India	4 291	13.7	9.0
Japan	2 675	8.5	5.6
South Korea	765	2.4	1.6
Turkey	625	2.0	1.3
Other	984	3.1	2.0
North and Central America	8 010	100.0	16.8
United States	6 575	82.1	13.8
Canada	793	9.9	1.7
Mexico	573	7.2	1.2
Other	69	0.9	0.1
Western and Eastern Europe	5 480	100.0	11.5
Spain	1 196	21.8	2.5
France	569	10.4	1.2
Italy	524	9.6	1.1
United Kingdom	517	9.4	1.1
Other	2 674	48.8	5.6
Africa	1 269	100.0	2.7
South Africa	539	42.5	1.1
Other	730	57.5	1.5
South America	979	100.0	2.1
Brazil	594	60.7	1.3
Other	385	39.3	0.8
Austral-Asia	577	100.0	1.2
Australia	486	84.2	1.0
Other	91	15.8	0.1
Total	47 655	NA	100.0

Source: World Commission on Dams, 2000.

These dams produce a combined 2643 TWh (terawatt-hours) of electricity annually, which represents just over 18 per cent of their technically feasible generating capacity of 14 370 TWh. These dams average just over 100 feet (31 metres) in height, have an average reservoir area of 63 300 square feet (23 square kilometres) and have an average reservoir capacity of 20 247 acre-feet (269 million cubic metres). Dams in Asia and North and Central America account for over one-half of world hydroelectric generation, producing 1453 TWh of hydroelectric power annually. An additional 1086 TWh of hydroelectric power is divided almost equally between European and South American dams. Dams in Africa and Austral-Asia produce the final 104 TWh of electricity.

According to the United States Department of Energy, the largest producers of hydroelectric power are the United States and Canada, which together account for nearly 700 billion kilowatt-hours (kWh) of hydroelectricity generation. Brazil produces an additional 250 billion kWh and China generates about 175 billion kWh of hydroelectric power. The next largest hydroelectric power generating countries are (in order of hydroelectric power output) Russia, Norway, Japan, India, France and Venezuela.

Most large dams serve one (or more) of the following purposes: irrigation, water supply, flood control and hydroelectric power generation. Interestingly, the use of the dams varies by region of the world. One-third of European dams, for example, are used to generate hydroelectric power, with another 20 per cent being used for irrigation. Nearly two-thirds of Asian dams are for irrigation, with only 7 per cent being used for hydroelectricity generation. In North and Central America, dam use is almost equally divided between irrigation, hydroelectric power generation, water supply, flood control and recreation. Nearly one-quarter of South American dams are used for hydroelectricity generation. For Africa, one-half of the dams are used for irrigation and another 20 percent are used for water supply. Finally, nearly one–half of the dams in Austral-Asia are used for water supply while 20 per cent are used for hydroelectric power generation. Table 2.2 summarizes the geographic distribution of dams by purpose.

Table 2.2 Breakdown of large dams by purpose and region (% by region)

	Western and Eastern Europe	Asia	North and Central America	South America	Africa	Austral-Asia
Flood control	3	2	13	18	1	2
Hydro-power	33	7	11	24	6	20
Irriga-tion	19	63	11	15	50	13
Multi-purpose	25	26	40	26	21	14
Recrea-tion	0	0	9	0	0	0
Water supply	17	2	10	13	20	49
Other	3	0	6	4	2	2

Source: World Commission on Dams, 2000.

2.4 SUMMARY AND CONCLUSIONS

This chapter has presented a historical overview of dams and hydroelectric power generation, discussed the history of how hydroelectric power generation is regulated in the United States, discussed how dams are distributed between different countries, and summarized how dam use varies between countries. In the next chapter, we present an overview of natural resource economics, which will serve as a backdrop for the more analytical material that will be presented in later chapters.

3. An overview of natural resource economics

This book adopts the point of view that dams and hydroelectricity generating facilities are best viewed from a broader water resource management backdrop. To this end, this chapter presents an overview of natural resource economics to provide the reader with the tools necessary to understand the material presented in later chapters. This chapter will divide the discussion of natural resource economics into exhaustible and renewable resource economics. For each type of resource, we present a simple dynamic model of how much of each resource to extract in each period. For exhaustible resources, we will derive the basic Hotelling (1931) rule which states that over time, the price of the resource will rise with the rate of interest and will become exhausted in the final period of a simple finite-horizon optimal control problem. For renewable resources, we will derive a fundamental capital-theoretic condition that governs the rate at which the resource will be harvested and determines the size of the resource stock in a steady-state. We will also present and discuss the notion of common-property resources, which causes economic rents to be dissipated as the resource is over-utilized. Given the elementary nature of the natural resource economics presented in this chapter, the reader familiar with this literature can easily skip this material and go on to the next chapter without any loss of continuity.

3.1 AN OVERVIEW OF EXHAUSTIBLE AND RENEWABLE RESOURCE ECONOMICS

As we will discuss in more detail in Chapter 4, hydroelectric power is generated by allowing water to pass through turbines located inside a dam. This means that managing a hydroelectric facility involves making decisions about how water is to be used in this manner in each period. Like any input in the production of any good or service, the water used to generate electricity has alternative uses. The water can remain in the reservoir behind the dam to be used for crop irrigation, municipal water supply, to support recreational activities such as boating or fishing, or can have other uses. While these alternative uses of water are often viewed in purely static terms, we can also consider the alternative uses of water in a dynamic context. For virtually all dams, water is replenished through inflows to the reservoir from rivers, streams and other sources and it is in this sense that hydroelectric power is often classified as a renewable resource. However, the rate at which water flows into a reservoir will depend on many factors, including existing hydrological conditions and releases from upstream dams. In some cases, the rate at which water will flow into a reservoir is uncertain. At other times, inflows into a reservoir can be determined from water releases from upstream dams. In addition, and as we shall see in Chapter 4, the amount of water in the reservoir will affect how much electricity will be generated when the water is released. What we shall find is that *ceteris paribus*, the more water in a reservoir, the more power will be generated per unit of water released.

Thus, the manager of the hydroelectricity facility must consider these factors in deciding when to release water and how much water to release in each period. Moreover, the water continues to have uses even after it is released, and many operating plans, which dictate water release rates from dams, will include consideration of what we will refer to as downstream water uses. As a result of these considerations, the economics of dam management in general, and hydroelectric power generation in particular, is best couched in natural resource economics terms, and hence we begin our discussion of the basics of natural resource economics.

3.2   THE ECONOMIC THEORY OF EXHAUSTIBLE RESOURCES

We begin our discussion of natural resource economics by first considering a resource that is extracted for some purpose. We can think of this resource as oil that is extracted from a well, as some mineral that is extracted from a mine or quarry. What is important at this point is that the resource is exhaustible, namely, once the resource is extracted, there is less available for future extraction within a reasonable period of time. Let us denote the stock in time period t as $X(t)$. For the sake of simplicity, we assume that the initial stock of the resource in period 0 is known and equal to $X(0) = S$. In each period, a decision is made of how much of this resource to extract (or harvest). Let us denote the amount extracted in each period t as $x(t)$ and we assume that in each period $x(t) \geq 0$. Of particular interest to us is the rate at which stock of the resource changes from period to period as it is extracted. We denote the rate at which the resource is extracted as:

$$\dot{X} = dX_t / dt \qquad (3.1)$$

where the term $\dot{X}$ refers to the derivative of $X(t)$ with respect to time period t. It turns out that since the source is exhaustible, the rate of change in the stock of the resource will also equal the rate at which the resource is extracted, so we modify equation (3.1) above to include extraction, which yields equation (3.2) below:

$$\dot{X} = -x(t) \qquad (3.2)$$

Naturally, when we think of the variable $X(t)$ representing the stock of the resource in period t as the stock variable in our system, we can also think of the variable $x(t)$ as the flow variable in our system. In this context, we will refer to equation (3.2) as our equation of motion, which governs how the stock of the resource will change over time as the resource is extracted. The equation of motion will be an important part of all of the models that we present in later chapters.

The decision-maker in this example must decide how much of the resource to extract in each period. Extracting more of the resource now will certainly yield higher immediate benefits, but will also reduce the amount of the resource available for future extraction. For the sake of simplicity, we assume that the resource is used (or sold) immediately upon extraction and has no other uses once it is extracted. We also assume that once extracted, the resource is sold in competitive markets at a price of $p(t)$ per period. We can think of the seller as being too small, relative to the rest of the industry, to have any appreciable influence on market price. Thus, in each period, the decision-maker is a price-taker and receives total revenues equal to $p(t)x(t)$. In our simple model, we also assume that future prices are known with certainty. More realistic exhaustible resource models, of course, address the issue of uncertainty with respect to price and other variables of importance. The reader is referred to Pindyck (1980) and Arrow and Chang (1982) for two articles that address the issue of uncertainty with respect to exhaustible resources.

Nevertheless, the basic economic problem confronting our resource harvester is to decide how much of the resource to extract in each period. Moreover, in our simple model, the decision of how much of the resource to extract in each period is to be made now, that is, in advance of these future periods. Somehow, the decision-maker must weigh the returns that are going to accrue in different periods from extracting the resource in different periods, which means that the resource owner must be able to compare the returns from extracting the resource in the different periods. The solution to this dilemma is discounting. As is well known in the economics literature, agents prefer current consumption over future consumption and will therefore discount the future when making decisions involving trade-offs between present and future consumption. For example, suppose someone is offered the opportunity of receiving $1 now plus $1 one year from now with complete certainty (and even zero inflation). How much would this individual be willing to pay now for such an offer? Even though the total return is $2, it's unlikely any individual would be willing to pay $2 for this opportunity. Even though paying $2 now yields an immediate (and certain) return of $1 and a certain pay-off of an additional $1 one year from now, the individual still foregoes the services of the second dollar for one year. In deciding how much this individual would pay for this opportunity, it is necessary to convert the dollar to be earned one year from now into terms that make this individual indifferent between having the second dollar now and receiving the second dollar one year from now. This conversion is done by applying a discount factor to the second dollar. This discount factor (for one year) is simply equal to one plus the discount rate. If this discount rate is 10 per cent, the discount factor would then be 1.10. Dividing this discount factor into the $1 to be received one year from now yields approximately $0.91. Adding the $1 to be received now to the $0.91 yields $1.91, which represents the most this individual would be willing to pay now for the option of receiving the $1 now and one additional dollar one year from now. Thus, this $1.91 figure then represents what is known as the discounted present value of the stream of income consisting of $1 now and $1 one year from now.

Since most natural resource economics problems extend into more than one future period, we often have to apply the notion of discounting to streams of income that extend beyond one future period. If there are $t=1,...,T$ future periods, then there will be T discount factors, each one of which will be applied to the return received in each of the T years. For the tth period, the discount factor will be $1/(1+i)^t$. As a result, a stream of income I_t to be received in each of the T periods in the future will have a discounted present value of $\sum_{t=1}^{T} I_t/(1+i)^t$. For the problems that we will consider in this book, we will assume that the decision-maker will discount the future at the rate i and that this discount rate does not change over the time horizon of the problem. As a result, the basic problem that the decision-maker will face will be to choose values of some decision variable that maximizes the discounted present value of a stream of future returns subject to constraints including those on resource availability, technology and operating flexibility.

3.2.1 EXTRACTING AN EXHAUSTIBLE RESOURCE WITH ZERO EXTRACTION COSTS

For our first natural resource model, we assume that harvesting or mining costs are zero. In this case, net receipts in period t are given by:

$$\pi_t = p(t)x(t) \tag{3.3}$$

The decision-maker cannot choose just any rate of extraction. The decision-maker faces a constraint on how much of the resource is available. We represent this constraint by the equation of motion given in equation (3.2) above. We also assume that extraction rates are bounded by

$$x_{min} \leq x(t) \leq x_{max} \qquad (3.4)$$

We can easily think of $x_{min} \geq 0$ (we cannot extract negative amounts of the resource) and we face some constraint on production capacity (we can only pump so much oil out of a well in any period) so that $x(t) \leq x_{max}$. In later chapters, our hypothetical dam operator will be constrained by hourly water release restrictions not unlike those given in equation (3.4). In these cases, the operator will be required to release at least some amount of water in each period to meet downstream water use requirements. Maximum hourly water release constraints will exist due to generator capacity or due to environmental restrictions intended to limit the degree of hourly fluctuations in water release rates. In any case, we assume that the decision-maker decides how much of the resource to extract in each period until the resource is exhausted. More formally, the decision-maker will decide on how much of the resource to extract in each period t (which goes from 1 to T) in order to maximize the discounted present value of profits.

The decision–maker will choose rates of extraction in each period to maximize the discounted present value of profits, subject to the equation of motion (3.2). If we assume a continuous-time problem, the objective is then to maximize:

$$Max\,PV = \int_0^\infty e^{-it} p(t)x(t)dt \qquad (3.5)$$

subject to the equation of motion (3.2) and equation (3.4). Solving this problem is facilitated by setting up the following Hamiltonian:

$$H = p(t)x(t) + \lambda(t)[-x(t)] \qquad (3.6)$$

To keep our discussion simple, we shall assume that the constraint in equation (3.4) is met already, so we do not include it explicitly in equation (3.6). Maximizing equation (3.6) with respect to the rate of extraction, our control variable, yields the following first-order condition (and suppressing the time subscript to ease the notational burden):

$$\frac{\partial H}{\partial x} = p - \lambda = 0 \tag{3.7}$$

The λ that appears in equations (3.6) and (3.7) is a function that is sometimes referred to as the 'adjoint' variable. For the problem at hand, the maximum principle tells us that there will exist an adjoint variable, in this case λ, such that the following adjoint equation is satisfied:

$$\dot{\lambda} = i\lambda - \partial H / \partial X = i\lambda = 0 \Rightarrow i = \frac{\dot{\lambda}}{\lambda} \tag{3.8}$$

Taking time derivatives of equation (3.7) and substituting the results into equation (3.8) yields the following result:

$$\frac{\dot{p}}{p} = i \tag{3.9}$$

This equation is the Hotelling (1931) result that says that the price of the resource rises at the rate of interest. In a finite-time problem, the resource would be exhausted at a rate where the price rose over time according to equation (3.9), but would also be exhausted at a rate that ensured that the resource was depleted by the end of the last period. In this example, we can envisage the existence of a choke price that would be reached in the last period as the resource is depleted. At this price, $\bar{p}$, the quantity demanded of the resource is zero. Figures 3.1 and 3.2 illustrate this example in a finite-time optimal control problem with an exhaustible resource. In the very first period, we start with X_0 of the resource which sells initially at a price of p_0. Over time, the resource will be depleted as it is used up and the price will rise with the rate of interest (according to equation 3.9). We illustrate the behaviour of the resource price in Figure 3.1. In Figure 3.2, we illustrate how the stock of the resource changes as it is extracted over time. Note that the choke price is reached just at the time that the resource stock is depleted, a result that can be gleaned by comparing the two figures together.

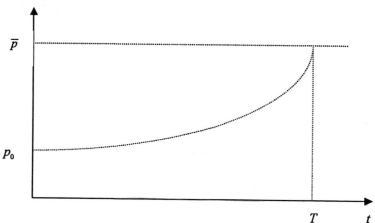

Figure 3.1 Price path in exhaustible resource example

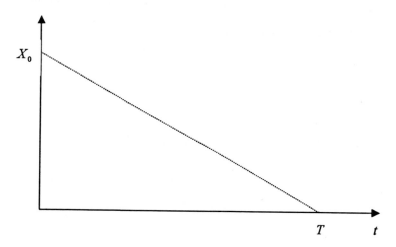

Figure 3.2 Resource stock path in exhaustible resource example

3.2.2   EXTRACTING AN EXHAUSTIBLE RESOURCE WITH POSITIVE HARVESTING COSTS

If we introduce harvesting costs into the model, we get slightly different results that admit a somewhat richer economic interpretation. In this case, we assume that extracting the resource requires the use of other resources, which we can think of as capital and labour. For our purposes, we shall assume that extraction costs in period t depend on the rate of extraction and the existing stock of the resource in period t. We express this cost function as $c = c(x(t), X(t))$. We assume that this cost function is twice–continuously differentiable in both $x(t)$ and $X(t)$. We assume that c is increasing in $x(t)$ and decreasing in $X(t)$. If we want to extract the resource at a faster rate, we will have to bear higher costs. If we have more of the resource to harvest, extraction costs are lower. We also assume that marginal extraction costs are increasing with the rate of extraction. However, for a given rate of extraction, marginal costs decrease with a larger resource stock and rise with a smaller resource stock. In other words, we assume that extraction costs increase at an increasing rate as the rate of extraction increases, and that extraction costs increase at an increasing rate as the resource is depleted.

Under these assumptions, the objective is to maximize:

$$Max\,PV = \int_0^\infty e^{-it}[p(t)x(t) - c(x(t), X(t))]dt \qquad (3.10)$$

subject to equations (3.2) and (3.4). The resulting Hamiltonian function is:

$$H = p(t)x(t) - c(x(t), X(t)) + \lambda[-x(t)] \qquad (3.11)$$

This equation is maximized with respect to the control variable, $x(t)$. The first-order condition on the control is:

$$\frac{\partial H}{\partial x} = p - \partial c/\partial x - \lambda = 0 \qquad (3.12)$$

The adjoint equation is given by:

$$\dot{\lambda} = i\lambda - \partial H/\partial X = i\lambda + \partial c/\partial X = 0 \qquad (3.13)$$

The above two equations can be combined to form the following fairly common equation that establishes the trade-off between present and future consumption of the exhaustible resource.

$$i = -\frac{\partial c/\partial X}{p - \partial c/\partial x} \qquad (3.14)$$

The numerator of the right-hand side of the above equation captures the effect that larger resource stocks have on harvesting costs. A larger resource stock, *ceteris paribus*, reduces harvesting costs so the numerator is negative. More important, reducing the stock of the resource through harvesting increases the costs of harvesting additional units of the resource. This term can then be thought of as capturing the impact that reducing the stock has on harvesting costs. When more of the resource is extracted in the current period, this leaves less of the resource available in future periods which also means that harvesting costs in the future will be higher. This means that we can interpret this denominator as the opportunity cost of the resource. If you harvest the resource now, you will incur higher harvesting costs in the future. Put differently, if you leave an additional unit of the resource unharvested in the current period, you face lower harvesting costs in the future. Since the denominator of the right-hand side of equation (3.12) is the net return to harvesting an additional unit of the resource in the current period, equation (3.12) says that the optimal rate of extraction, x_t^*, will be chosen so as to equate the benefits of harvesting the resource in the current periods with the discounted present value of the opportunity cost of harvesting the resource.

3.3   THE ECONOMIC THEORY OF RENEWABLE RESOURCES

The foregoing analysis is based on a resource whose stock does not replenish over time. We now turn to the case of a resource whose stock can grow over time. We can easily think of this resource as a stock of a particular species of fish, but we can just as easily think of the resource as a forest, a population of deer or any other life that grows over time. The resource will be assumed to grow according to the function $F(X(t))$. For our purposes, it is not necessary to delve into all of the technical details of the behaviour of this growth function. Typically, this function is assumed to be twice–continuously differentiable in $X(t)$. However, this function will not generally be increasing in $X(t)$ for all values of $X(t)$. For example, a quadratic form of F would have growth initially increasing in $X(t)$, but once a certain population size is reached, growth could actually decline as $X(t)$ increases. We can think of this as a case of crowding, where larger numbers of fish compete for the same limited food supplies and hence grow at a slower rate. In addition to the natural growth of the population, we also allow harvesting of $X(t)$, which offsets any natural growth that occurs with the population in question. Adding harvest in each period, which we denote by $x(t)$, yielding the following growth function for the stock of our renewable resource:

$$\frac{dX(t)}{dt} = \dot{X} = F(X(t)) - x(t) \qquad (3.15)$$

We can illustrate population growth in Figure 3.3. In the absence of harvesting, this growth function assumes very stylized population growth that may not be consistent with many renewable resources in the real world, namely, that population growth is quadratic. Under this specification, resource growth will fall to zero if the stock of the resource falls to (or below) some lower limit ($\underline{X}$). Resource growth will also fall to zero when the resource stock reaches the carrying capacity of the environment (at a stock of $\overline{X}$). Both of these stock levels represent stationary points on this growth function, but the lower limit, $\underline{X}$, represents an unstable point. At a stock of $\hat{X}$, the resource grows at the maximum rate. Later on, we will modify this graph to include the effects of harvesting. Ideally, we will be able to arrive at a rate of harvesting that allows the resource to be sustainable, that is, a steady-state where the growth in the resource, net of harvesting, is zero. The reader is referred to Dasgupta and Heal (1979) and Clark (1976) for more detailed examples and discussions of population growth models.

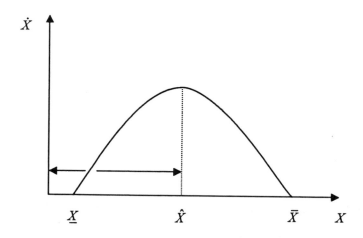

Figure 3.3   Population growth in simple renewable resource model

We now turn to harvesting the resource. In this simple model, we assume that the harvested resource is sold in competitive markets at a price p in each period t. The decision-maker makes a decision analogous to that in the previous section, namely, on rates of harvest in each period to maximize the discounted present value of net receipts. Moreover, the decision-maker confronts the same trade-off between present and future consumption as in the exhaustible resource case. In the renewable resource case, however, consuming more of the resource now involves forgoing the opportunity to harvest what would be available in future periods, after accounting for the growth in the resource. Nevertheless, the decision-maker will discount the future (again, at the rate of discount i). To this end, we set up the following constrained optimization problem:

$$Max\,PV = \int_0^\infty e^{-it}[p(t)x(t) - c(x(t), X(t))]dt \qquad (3.16)$$

subject to the equation of motion (3.15) and a constraint on per-period extraction rates analogous to that given in equation (3.4) above in the exhaustible resource case. As in the exhaustible resource case, we solve this problem by first setting up the appropriate Hamiltonian function:

$$H = p(t)x(t) - c(x(t), X(t)) + \lambda[F(X(t)) - x(t)] \qquad (3.17)$$

Again, maximizing equation (3.17) with respect to the rate of harvest yields the following first-order conditions on the control variable:

$$\frac{\partial H}{\partial x} = p - \partial c/\partial x - \lambda = 0 \qquad (3.18)$$

The adjoint equation is given by:

$$\dot{\lambda} = i\lambda - \partial H/\partial X = i\,\lambda + \partial c/\partial X - \partial F/\partial X = 0 \qquad (3.19)$$

If we assume a steady-state solution, where $\dot{\lambda} = 0$, we can combine equations (3.18) and (3.19) to yield the following:

$$p - \partial c/\partial x = \frac{1}{i}(\partial F/\partial X - \partial c/\partial X) \qquad (3.20)$$

This equation establishes a fairly well-known relationship that governs how the renewable resource manager will decide between current and future rates of harvest. As in the exhaustible resource case, the left-hand side of equation (3.20) is the net return to harvesting the resource in the current period. The right-hand side of equation (3.20) is the opportunity cost of harvesting the resource in the current period, namely, the discounted present value of the effects that harvesting now has on the future size of the resource as measured through its effects on future harvesting costs and resource growth. We can rearrange equation (3.20) to obtain the following:

$$i = \partial F / \partial X - \frac{\partial c / \partial X}{p - \partial c / \partial x} \tag{3.21}$$

This equation is analogous to that presented in Clark (1976) under a slightly different model specification, but the basic message remains. In the case where harvesting costs are independent of the size of the resource, $\partial c / \partial X = 0$, and equation (3.21) reduces to $i = \partial F / \partial X$. This simpler version of the equation says that harvesting will occur at a rate that equates the discount rate to the marginal productivity of the resource stock, which is analogous to the standard marginal productivity of capital rule. In the event that harvesting costs depend on the size of the resource, we have to take a closer look at the second term in the right-hand side of equation (3.21). Close inspection of this term reveals that it is negative, or:

$$\frac{\partial c / \partial X}{p - \partial c / \partial x} < 0 \tag{3.22}$$

This means that $i > \partial F / \partial X$ which implies that harvesting costs that depend on the stock of the resource increase the steady-state size of the stock.

We can illustrate static equilibrium graphically. To do so, we first assume that the harvest depends on a variable that reflects the input use by the harvester of the renewable resource, a variable that we shall call effort. We will further assume that we can express harvesting as a function of effort and the stock of the resource, namely as $h_t = h_t(X_t, E_t)$. We assume that this function is well behaved, namely that it is continuously differentiable in both arguments and has positive first-derivatives with respect to each of its arguments. If we substitute this into a discrete-time version of our population growth function, that is, a discrete-time version of equation (3.15) and evaluate this function at the steady-state stock level, say $\tilde{X}_t$, where $\dot{X}_t = 0$, then we will have $F(X_t)=h_t(X_t, E_t)$. If we can solve this last equation for X_t as a function of E_t, say $X_t = X_t(E_t)$, and substitute this into the production function, we will have what is known as a yield-effort function given by $h_t = h_t(X_t(E_t), E_t) = h_t(E_t)$. This function shows the relationship between harvest and effort in a steady–state.

Where all of this is heading is a modified version of Figure 3.3 that incorporates prices, costs and effort into the analysis of decision-making for a renewable resource. Recall that Figure 3.3 expressed growth as a function of the stock of the resource. If we solve this growth function for the steady-state stock of the resource as a function of effort, and substitute this into our harvesting function, we will obtain an analogue to Figure 3.3 that measures yield against effort.

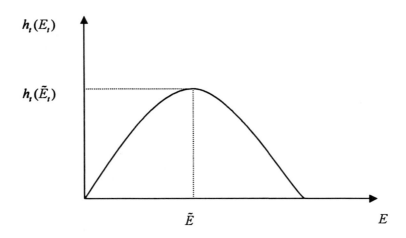

Figure 3.4 The yield–effort function

In Figure 3.4, the maximum sustainable yield is that level of harvest associated with the level of effort $\tilde{E}_t$. To turn this into more of an economic model we have to introduce revenues and costs. If the harvest is sold in competitive markets at a constant price p_t, then total revenues can be expressed as $R_t = p_t h_t(E_t)$, which is represented in Figure 3.5 below. If we represent harvesting costs as a simple linear function of effort, then costs can be represented by the equation $C_t = c_t E_t$, which we include in Figure 3.5.

Figure 3.5 shows what looks like two equilibria, one at E_0 and one at E_1. However, there is an important distinction between these two levels of effort. The first equilibrium level of effort, E_0, represents what is referred to as the Rent Maximizing Effort and represents that level of effort that corresponds to setting effort where marginal revenue equals marginal cost. If we assume, however, that access to the resource is open (such as in the case of the open-access fishery), we see that this initial equilibrium will not be sustained. Entry will continue to occur (and hence effort will increase) until profits are driven to zero. This occurs at the second equilibrium, where total revenues equal total costs and effort equals E_1. The foregoing is the standard open-access fishery argument presented by Gordon (1954) and Scott (1955). We have referred to Clark (1976) elsewhere in this chapter, but there are plenty of other articles that address fishery economics and fisheries management. A small sample includes papers by Beverton and Holt (1957), Burt and Cummings (1970), Christy and Scott (1965), Crutchfield and Zellner (1962), Turvey (1964), Smith (1968), Plourde (1970) and Brown (1974). The reader is also referred to Anderson (1986) for a more complete discussion of fishery economics. The volume edited by Mirman and Spulber (1982) contains many articles on renewable resources. While it is easy to use fish as an example of a renewable resource, there is a considerable literature on the economics of forestry. A very small sampling of that literature includes Johansson and Löfgren (1985), Samuelson (1976), Hartman (1976) and Deacon (1985).

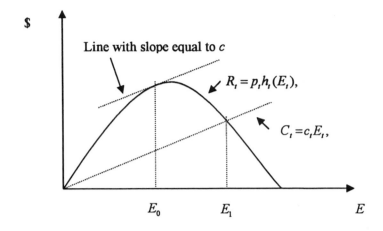

Figure 3.5 Open access and rent maximizing levels of effort

This concludes our introduction to, and summary of, the basics of natural resource economics. As we shall see in later chapters, the water used to generate hydroelectric power has the characteristics of both an exhaustible and a renewable resource. It is an exhaustible resource in the sense that once the water is used to generate power, it cannot be used again for future generation (save for examples of pumped storage). In addition, many operating plans that govern the generation of hydroelectricity require that fixed quantities of water be released over a given period, for example, one month. This suggests that in any given period, the water available for generation can be treated as being fixed in quantity. One of the constraints facing the dam operator is then to decide how best to use this fixed allocation of water over the course of a one-month interval. On the other hand, hydroelectric power is generally classified as a renewable resource. While not attempting to instigate a debate over semantics, this classification is somewhat misleading. The water does not by itself regenerate as would trees, fish or other more traditional renewable resources. The 'growth' of water in a reservoir cannot be modelled in the same sense that a population of deer can be modelled (with the amount of growth depending on the size of the stock). However, the supply of water is indeed replenished, partly through the hydrological cycle and, as long as additional water supplies are forthcoming, the resource can be treated as one having at least some of the characteristics of renewable resources.

3.4   SUMMARY AND CONCLUSIONS

In this chapter, we have presented an overview of natural resource economics. We have followed the tradition of dividing natural resource economics into two categories: exhaustible and renewable resources. For each type of resource, we presented a simple dynamic model which involved making decisions on how much of a resource to extract in each period of a multi-period problem. For exhaustible resources, we derived the basic Hotelling rule which states that over time, the price of the resource will rise with the rate of interest and will become exhausted in the final period of a simple finite-horizon optimal control problem. For renewable resources, we derived a fundamental capital-theoretic condition that governs the rate at which the resource will be harvested and the size of the resource stock in a steady-state. We also introduced the notion of a common-property resource, which causes economic rents to be dissipated as the resource is over-utilized.

The next chapter has more background material that will prove useful in later chapters, namely, the mechanics of dams, that is, how dams function the way that they do. This will be an important foundation for the material that follows. This chapter will emphasize the dual roles that water plays in hydroelectric power generation, namely how the flows of water as released from a dam generate hydroelectric power and how the stock of water stored behind the dam contributes to both current and future rates of hydroelectricity generation.

4. How they work

What is hydroelectric power and where does it come from? How is hydroelectric power generated? What factors determine how much hydroelectric power an individual dam generates? Where does the water used for hydroelectricity generation come from and where does this water go after it has been used to generate power? How does hydroelectric power get from the point of generation to consumers? Is hydroelectricity generation the only thing dams are used for? The answers to these and many other questions are the subject of this chapter. We will begin this chapter with a discussion of the hydrologic cycle, which ultimately provides the water used for hydroelectric power generation. We will then discuss the mechanics of dam construction and operation and discuss the fundamental engineering principles behind hydroelectric power generation. We will also present a more formal model of hydroelectricity generation, a model that will form the basis for the economic models presented in later chapters.

4.1 THE HYDROLOGIC CYCLE

Hydroelectric power is generated by the force of water as it falls from behind a dam through devices called turbines. The force of the falling water causes these turbines to spin and, in turn, generate what we call hydroelectric power. But where does the water come from and how does it return to the reservoir once it has been released? It turns out that the amount of water that we use today (for all purposes) has been here for hundreds of millions of years and the amount of water available today is probably the same as it was then. What has happened over the years, and continues to happen to this day, is described by what is called the hydrologic cycle. The hydrologic cycle is made up of five processes: condensation, precipitation, infiltration, run-off and evapotranspiration. In short, water vapours condense to form clouds which cause precipitation. The precipitation falls to the earth and infiltrates the soil or flows to the ocean as run-off. Water stored in the ocean, lakes, streams, rivers and so on (surface water) then evaporates which returns the moisture to the atmosphere. Plants return water to the atmosphere through a process called transpiration. Figure 4.1 illustrates the hydrologic cycle.

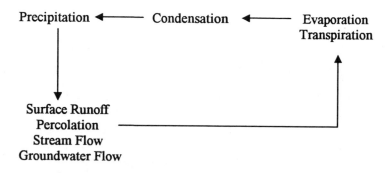

Figure 4.1 The hydrologic cycle

4.2   GENERATING HYDROELECTRIC POWER

Since energy can neither be created nor destroyed, hydroelectric generation can be viewed as a process of converting one form of energy into another. The generation of hydroelectric power involves no less than three such conversions. Energy based on motion is referred to as kinetic energy. Hydroelectric power ultimately comes from the kinetic energy embodied in the movement of water through generators. However, before the kinetic energy contained in the moving water is converted into hydroelectric power, it must first be converted from kinetic energy into mechanical energy. Mechanical energy is simply energy created by a machine. The process of generating hydroelectric power involves converting the energy contained in moving water (the kinetic energy) into the mechanical energy created by the turbines that spin a generator rotor. The final act of energy conversion is from mechanical to electrical energy, which comes from the water spinning the rotor in the generator. Since water is the initial source of this electricity, we refer to the electricity generated by this process as hydroelectric power.

It does not take a lot of water to generate hydroelectric power. Hydroelectric plants can be as small as 100 kilowatts, which the United States Department of Energy refers to as micro hydropower. Large hydropower, which is emphasized in this book, refers to facilities having generating capacities exceeding 30 megawatts. Nevertheless, what is required to generate hydroelectric power are sufficient quantities of moving water available and the ability to harness this water for generation. Generally, there are three types of hydroelectric power facilities. Impoundment facilities, which will form the basis for much of the hydroelectric power discussed in this book, uses a dam to store water in a reservoir. Hydroelectric power is generated when water is released from the dam through its penstocks to flow through the generators. Impoundment facilities perhaps represent the most flexible and reliable arrangement and involve the use of dams that allow water to be stored for release when the hydroelectric power is needed. In fact, hydroelectric power represents just about the only way in which electricity can be stored, but in this case, the electricity is 'stored' as water behind the dam which is then 'used' when it is released from behind the dam to pass through the generators and is converted into electricity. Diversion facilities are located on rivers, streams and canals. These facilities divert water through a penstock or a canal to generate electricity. Pumped storage facilities are so named because they can pump water from a lower reservoir to an upper reservoir for generation when needed. One of the advantages of pumped storage facilities is that they can pump water into the upper reservoir during off-peak periods, when electricity rates and demand are typically lower, for release and generation during on-peak periods.

The water stored behind dams often serves purposes other than hydroelectric power generation. As discussed in Chapters 1 and 2, dams also allow water to be stored for many purposes, including flood control and irrigation. The water stored behind dams can also be used for domestic and industrial uses and support such recreational activities as swimming, boating and fishing. In the United States, for example, roughly 2 per cent of the dams are actually used for hydroelectric power generation.

Figure 4.2 illustrates a generic hydroelectric generating facility. Water is stored behind the dam in what is called a forebay. The quantity of water in the forebay can be expressed in terms of acre-feet of volume, but can also be measured in terms of elevation, which refers to the number of feet the surface of the reservoir is above sea level. This is important because the elevation of the reservoir will determine an important attribute of a dam that has a direct bearing on the amount of hydroelectric power that can be generated. This attribute is the head of the dam, which refers to the distance between the elevation of the reservoir and the top of the penstock, which is a tube through which water flows to the generator. The higher the head, the faster the water will fall through the penstocks and hence the greater the amount of kinetic energy that the generator will eventually convert into electrical energy.

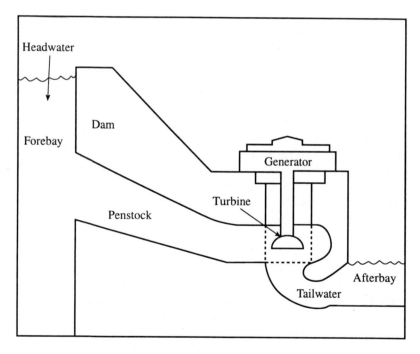

Figure 4.2 Diagram of a dam
Source: US Department of the Interior, Bureau of Reclamation, 2001.

When water is released for generation, the water will fall from the forebay through the penstock to the turbines, which are spun by the flow of water. The spinning of the turbines causes rotors inside the generator to spin and generate electricity. The water will then flow into the afterbay of the dam and eventually flow downstream in a river connected to the afterbay. The hydroelectric power is then sent to the transmission grid for distribution for eventual consumption by households and other end-users.

The head of the dam is important for another reason, namely, the head affects the optimal selection of the turbine used for generation. The Pelton turbine is typically used for higher-head dams (ranging from 50 to 6000 feet) having a generating capacity of up to 200 megawatts. The Francis turbine is typically used for medium-head dams (ranging from 10 to 2000 feet) having a generating capacity as large as 800 megawatts. Finally, a propeller turbine is typically used on low head dams (ranging from 10 to 300 feet) and having a generating capacity of 100 megawatts. A special example of a propeller turbine is a Kaplan turbine which that has blades that can vary in pitch to optimize performance. Kaplan turbines allow for generating capacities of up to 400 megawatts.

To illustrate some of the concepts presented in this section, Table 4.1 contains actual data for Glen Canyon dam for a 24–hour period. For each hour of the day, the table shows the elevation of the dam (the height that the surface of the reservoir is above sea level), the tail and head of the dam, hourly water release rates and hydroelectricity generation. On this particular day, no spillage occurred nor were there any bypass releases (releases that flow from the reservoir into the afterbay but do not generate any hydroelectric power), so we exclude these data. We also show the ramping rate, that is, how much the water release rate changes between hours.

What we do not have data on inflows or content. If we had either of these, we could estimate inflows into the reservoir and construct a simple model that describes the dynamics of this particular dam. Nevertheless, one should notice the pattern of hourly water releases and resulting hydroelectricity generation. In the earlier parts of the day, water release rates and hence hydroelectricity generation are relatively low. As we move further into the day, and presumably as system load increases, water releases increase, as does hydroelectricity generation. As the day progresses from afternoon into evening, and as system load decreases, hourly water release rates drop off. Over the same interval, hydroelectric generation drops off to just about its early-morning rate. Finally, notice the ramping rates in the last column. These show how much the water release rates change from hour to hour, and show that there can be some rather dramatic changes in release rates over the course of the day.

Table 4.1 Hourly dam operations: Glen Canyon dam, 8 April 2002

Hour	Elevation (feet)	Tail (feet)	Head (feet)	Generation (MW)	Power release (CFS)	Ramp rate (CFS)
01:00	3 647.30	3 133.91	513.39	281	7 400	N/A
02:00	3 647.28	3 133.97	513.31	284	7 480	80
03:00	3 647.25	3 134.12	513.13	288	7 590	110
04:00	3 647.25	3 134.48	512.77	324	8 530	940
05:00	3 647.26	3 134.79	512.47	333	8 770	240
06:00	3 647.27	3 135.34	511.93	379	9 980	1 210
07:00	3 647.26	3 135.65	511.61	400	10 540	560
08:00	3 647.28	3 136.11	511.17	434	11 430	890
09:00	3 647.29	3 135.99	511.30	433	11 400	−30
10:00	3 647.29	3 135.99	511.30	433	11 400	0
11:00	3 647.28	3 135.98	511.30	426	11 220	−180
12:00	3 647.25	3 135.69	511.56	410	10 800	−420
13:00	3 647.24	3 135.40	511.84	410	10 800	0
14:00	3 647.25	3 135.53	511.72	776	20 440	9 640
15:00	3 647.26	3 135.49	511.77	387	10 190	−10 250
16:00	3 647.27	3 135.43	511.84	389	10 250	60
17:00	3 647.25	3 135.97	511.28	423	11 140	890
18:00	3 647.24	3 136.34	510.90	465	12 250	1 110
19:00	3 647.22	3 136.70	510.52	506	13 330	1 080
20:00	3 647.21	3 136.64	510.57	507	13 360	30
21:00	3 647.19	3 136.04	511.15	449	11 830	−1 530
22:00	3 647.20	3 135.59	511.61	395	10 410	−1 420
23:00	3 647.21	3 134.77	512.44	340	8 960	−1 450
24:00	3 647.23	3 134.57	512.66	330	8 690	−270

Source: Western Area Power Administration.

Figure 4.4 shows hydroelectricity generation over the same 24-hour period. Naturally, the pattern of hourly hydroelectricity generation follows the hourly pattern of water release rates. We illustrate some of the patterns in the following Figures 4.3 and 4.4. Figure 4.3 shows water release and ramping rates over the course of the day. This figure show just how much the hourly water release rates can change over a short period of time. In later chapters, we will examine some of the operating restrictions that limit the flexibility of the hydroelectric facility operator, which will include restrictions that limit the rate at which water releases can change.

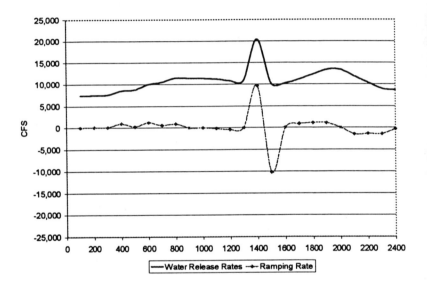

Figure 4.3 Water release and ramping rates: Glen Canyon dam, 8 April 2002

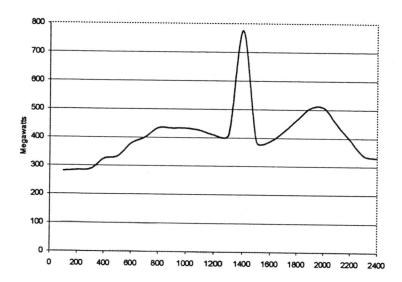

Figure 4.4 Hydroelectric generation: Glen Canyon dam, 8 April 2002

4.3   WHAT HAPPENS TO THE WATER?

After the water flows through the dam, it will flow down a river where it can either remain in the river system to support downstream ecosystems, can be diverted to other rivers and reservoirs, or can be used for agricultural, residential, industrial and other purposes.

While hydroelectric power can be generated without producing the emissions characteristic of coal- and gas-fired generation technologies, it can have other kinds of negative environmental effects. Water flowing down a river from a dam can cause erosion of downstream banks that, in turn, can affect the kinds of plant and animal life that inhabit the downstream environment. On some rivers, the placement of dams can inhibit the movement of fish, such as salmon, to their spawning areas, an impact that can have adverse effects on the long-term survival of fish species. Moreover, destruction of fish species can have negative impacts on recreational fishing.

4.4   AN INTRODUCTION TO HYDROELECTRIC GENERATION

The technical relationship between water release, dam head and generation can be described by the following equation:

$$q = \frac{CFS \cdot Head}{\alpha} \qquad (4.1)$$

where q is hydroelectric output, *CFS* is the water release rate and *Head* is the head of the dam. The coefficient α is a factor that converts the product of water releases and dam head to hydroelectric generation. A recent publication by the US Bureau of Reclamation (2001a) uses a value of $\alpha = 8.8$. However, the actual value of this coefficient can vary from facility to facility.

In the above equation, generation is expressed in terms of theoretical horsepower, but can be converted to watts of generation by multiplying generation by 746 (since one horsepower equals 746 watts). For example, suppose water is released at a rate of 5000 CFS from a dam with a 400-foot head. According to the above equation, this would generate 22 773 horsepower of electricity. Dividing this figure by 746 and converting (from watts to megawatts) yields 170 megawatts of hydroelectricity generation.

We take an alternate view of hydroelectricity generation in Figure 4.5. In this graph, we represent the relationship between water release, head and generation graphically by the isoquant. Each isoquant represents combinations of release rates, measured along the vertical axis and dam head, measured along the horizontal axis, that produce the same amount of electricity. For a given dam head, we can increase output by increasing the rate of water release. If we begin again at point A on the first isoquant, increasing the water release rate and maintaining the dam head allows us to move to point B on the higher isoquant.

The general downward slope of each isoquant captures the notion that hydroelectricity generation involves trade-offs between release rates and dam head. Suppose we are operating at point A on the first isoquant. If, for example, the head of the dam falls, the hydroelectric facility operator can compensate by increasing the rate at which water is released, thereby moving along the isoquant to maintain generation. In this example, we could maintain hydroelectric generation at the same level by moving to point C on the first isoquant.

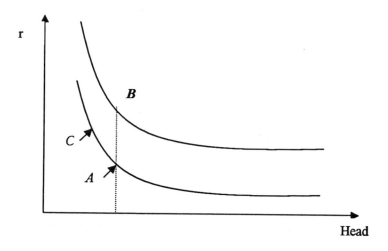

Figure 4.5 Hydroelectric power generation isoquant

The convex (to the origin) shape of the isoquants reflects the rate of substitution between these two inputs in the generation of hydroelectric power. As we move along an individual isoquant, increasing the rate of water release for smaller and smaller dam heads, we have to increase water release rates at an increasing rate for each equal reduction in dam head. Reconsider point A on the first isoquant. An initial reduction in dam head can be offset by an increase in the water release that brings us to point B. However, a further equivalent reduction in dam head requires a much greater increase in water release rates to main generation at the same level. In this example, we would move all the way from point B to point C. In effect, we are describing an increasing marginal rate of technical substitution between water release rates and dam head as we move north-west along the isoquant.

The above discussion has been presented in static terms. However, the relationships between water release rates, dam head and the rate of hydroelectric generation are inherently dynamic. Unless water releases are exactly offset by inflows to a reservoir, or pumped storage to return water to the upper reservoir of such facilities, continued water releases will eventually reduce the content of the reservoir, reducing the elevation of the reservoir and hence the head of the dam. With a lower dam head, maintaining the same rate of water releases can actually reduce hydroelectric generation. This head effect is captured directly in the production equation we have used in this section. However, unless the dam is quite small, water releases would have to be maintained for quite a few hours, if not days, without offsetting inflows to the reservoir, for these head effects to be significant. Nevertheless, water releases are planned by operators over the course of many days, if not weeks, and so these effects should be taken into account when water release rates are planned.

One of the purposes of this chapter is to emphasize that hydroelectric power generation is best viewed within the context of a broad set of water management issues. According to many of the statistics on dams presented earlier in this chapter, hydroelectric generation is but one of many uses of dams and, for many regions, hydroelectric power generation represents a small proportion of total dam use. In the model that we present below that describes the basic relationship between water releases and hydroelectricity generation, we take great care to ensure that we capture the effects that releasing water to generate hydroelectric power has on the remaining reservoir content and ultimate downstream flows. To accomplish this objective, we present the following four-equation model that describes hydroelectricity generation in terms of water release rates, but also captures the effects that reservoir levels have on reservoir content, dam elevation and dam head. The first equation is a production function that assumes that hydroelectric generation depends on the same two inputs that we discussed above, namely, water release rates and dam head. Specifically, we assume that hydroelectric generation in period t, given by q_t^h, depends on releases of water from the reservoir in period t, given by r_t, and the head of the dam in period t, h_t. This production function is given by the following equation:

$$q_t^h = q_t^h(r_t, h_t) \qquad (4.2)$$

We assume that this equation is continuously differentiable in both arguments, both first-derivatives are positive and both own second-derivatives are negative. We also assume that the cross-partial derivatives are positive. We assume $\partial^2 q_t^h / \partial r_t \partial h_t = \partial^2 q_t^h / \partial h_t \partial r_t > 0$. Accordingly, hydroelectric power generation is higher, for a given dam head, the higher the rate of water release. We also assume that hydroelectricity generation will be higher, the higher the dam head, for a given rate of water release. Moreover, we assume that both inputs are required to generate hydroelectric power. Thus, we assume that $q_t^h(0, h_t) = 0$ and that $q_t^h(r_t, 0) = 0$.

The effects that releasing water will ultimately have on dam head will be driven by two additional equations. The first of these two relates the dam head in period t to the elevation of the reservoir in period t. This equation is given by the following:

$$h_t = h_t(e_t) \tag{4.3}$$

where e_t is the elevation (in feet) of the reservoir in period t. The second of these two equations relates the elevation of the reservoir in period t to the amount of water in the reservoir in period t, given by the following:

$$e_t = e_t(w_t) \tag{4.4}$$

where w_t is the content of the reservoir (in acre-feet) in period t. We assume that equations (4.3) and (4.4) are increasing in their respective arguments. We also define the domain of this function to not exceed the capacity of the reservoir, so this function will be defined for values of w_t that are less than some threshold value, $\bar{w}_t$.

All else being equal, releasing water from a reservoir to generate hydroelectric power will reduce the content of that reservoir. To incorporate this, we complete our model with the following equation of motion, which describes how the stock of water changes when either releases or inflows to the reservoir change. Our equation of motion is given by the following:

$$w_t = w_{t-1} - r_{t-1} + f_{t-1} \qquad\qquad (4.5)$$

where f_t is the rate of inflow into the reservoir in period t. According to this equation, a steady-state exists when inflows equal releases, and hence $w_t = w_{t-1} \ \forall\, t$.

The above four equations will form the basis for most of the economic models of hydroelectric power provision presented in later chapters. We introduce these equations now to familiarize the reader with the basic water allocation issues involved in water management and hydroelectric power generation. Accordingly, releases of water to generate hydroelectric power will, to the extent that they are not completely offset by inflows to the reservoir, reduce the content of the reservoir (from equation 4.5). In turn, this will reduce the elevation of the reservoir (from equation 4.4). Reducing the elevation of the reservoir reduces the head of the dam (from equation 4.3). Finally, the rate of hydroelectric power generation is determined by the combination of water releases and dam head (from equation 4.2).

The above specification of hydroelectricity generation allows us to focus particular attention on the dual roles that water plays in the generation of hydroelectric power. The first role, which we term the flow value of water, refers to the direct contribution that releasing water in the current period makes to hydroelectric power generation in the current period. The second role, which we term the stock value of water, refers to the contribution that the stock of water contained in the reservoir makes to the head of the dam. For a given rate of water release, hydroelectric power generation will be higher, the larger the quantity of water in the reservoir. This suggests that the decision-maker should incorporate both of these factors in deciding how much water to release in each period.

In this model, we assume that the only use of water is for hydroelectricity generation. The water stored behind the dam could be used for residential or industrial purposes, or could be used to support recreational activities such as fishing or boating, behind the dam. We also assume that water is released for one purpose, namely, hydroelectric generation. The water that flows downstream could be used for many purposes, including industrial and agriculture consumption and could support downstream recreational activities such as river-rafting or fishing. Finally, the water could be used for additional generation by a hydraulically-coupled dam located downstream. We explore the issue of downstream generation in Chapters 8 and 9.

4.5   SUMMARY AND CONCLUSIONS

This chapter has presented an overview of how dams work. After presenting a brief overview of the hydrologic cycle, which governs how water is renewable, we illustrated how a dam functions. We then turned to the actual generation of hydroelectric power and developed the generation portion (that is, production function) of the model that will be used throughout the remaining chapters of this book. Of considerable importance are the dual roles that water plays in hydroelectricity generation, namely the stock and the flow values of water. This feature of hydroelectric power generation will play an important role in the models presented in later chapters.

5. An economic model of hydroelectric power provision

In this chapter we present two simple models of a hydroelectric generating facility. In the first model, the hydroelectric power dispatcher will decide how much water to release in each period in order to maximize profits. In the second model, hydroelectricity generation will be combined with thermal generation to provide power from these sources to maximize profits. In both models, conditions that define optimal rates of water release and optimal thermal electricity generation will be derived. In addition, the long-run dynamic properties of the model will be examined. The chapter will conclude with numerical examples that illustrate these results.

5.1 HYDROELECTRIC GENERATION

We begin with a somewhat simpler version of the model of hydroelectric power generation presented in the last chapter. In particular, we will simplify the relationship between dam elevation, content and head to include the content of the reservoir directly in the hydroelectric power production function. This means that hydroelectricity generation will be assumed to be governed by the following simpler version of equation (4.2) from the previous chapter:

$$q_t^h = q_t^h(r_t, W_t) \tag{5.1}$$

As before, hydroelectric power, q_t^h, is generated in period t by releasing water, r_t, in period t. The argument for reservoir content in the production function, W_t, will capture the combined effects that changes in content have on elevation, which in turn influences dam head, which finally influences the productivity of water releases. More formally, we express equation (4.2) as $q_t^h = \tilde{q}_t^h(r_t, h_t(e_t(W_t)))$. We successively substitute equations (4.3) and (4.4) to obtain equation (5.1).

Nevertheless, we make the same assumptions about equation (5.1) that we made about equation (4.2), namely, that it is continuously differentiable in both arguments, both first-derivatives are positive and both own second-derivatives are negative. Accordingly, hydroelectric generation will be higher, for a given dam content, the higher the rate of water release. We also assume that hydroelectric generation will be higher, the higher the dam content, for a given rate of water release.

Our simple model of hydroelectric generation will assume that the hydroelectric power dispatcher generates power and sells it in a large market. In particular, we assume that the hydroelectric power is sold in a market at a price given by the inverse demand function $p_t(Q_t)$ where Q_t represents the quantity of electricity sold during period t. We can express industry output as $Q_t = \tilde{Q}_t + q_t^h(r_t, W_t)$ where $\tilde{Q}_t$ represents power sold by the other generators or energy marketers serving this particular market. Moreover, we assume that water release costs behave according to the cost function, $c_t^h(r_t)$, which we assume to be continuously differentiable with positive first- and second-derivatives. Finally, we are solving this problem in discrete time. This allows us to think of each time period as lasting one hour, which allows us to address hourly time-of-day variations in prices and other variables that might influence the dispatcher's decisions. Under this set of assumptions, profits in each period to the dispatcher are given by the following equation:

$$\pi_t = p_t(Q_t)q_t^h(r_t, W_t) - c_t^h(r_t) \qquad (5.2)$$

The only constraints that the hydroelectric power operator faces in our simple model is an equation of motion, $W_t = W_{t-1} - r_{t-1} + f_{t-1}$, that is, equation (4.5) from the previous chapter, and a requirement that the dispatcher operate within the operating characteristics of the generator. For now, we will assume that the dispatcher satisfies this constraint. In the next chapter, we will introduce constraints on minimum and maximum release rates that are driven by environmental objectives. For the model presented in this chapter, however, we will not state these assumptions explicitly.

5.2   OPTIMAL PROVISION OF HYDROELECTRIC POWER

The dispatcher will choose rates of water release to maximize the discounted present value of profits subject to the equation of motion. The resulting Hamiltonian function is given by:

$$
\begin{aligned}
H = \sum_{t=1}^{T-1} \{ & p_t(Q_t)q_t^h(r_t,W_t) - c_t^h(r_t) + \gamma_{t+1}(W_{t+1} - W_t + r_t - f_t) \} \\
& + p_T(Q_T)q_T^h(r_T,W_T) - c_T^h(r_T) + \gamma_T(W_T + r_T - f_T)
\end{aligned} \tag{5.3}
$$

In the above equation, we define γ_{t+1} as the discrete-time costate associated with the equation of motion and define γ_T as the final period costate on the equation of motion. The first-order conditions on the control variable are given by:

$$
\frac{\partial H}{\partial r_t} = p_t \frac{\partial q_t^h}{\partial r_t} + \frac{\partial p_t}{\partial q_t^h} \frac{\partial q_t^h}{\partial r_t} q_t^h - \frac{\partial c_t^h}{\partial r_t} - \gamma_{t+1} \le 0 \tag{5.4}
$$

$$
r_t \frac{\partial H}{\partial r_t} = 0 \tag{5.5}
$$

Equations (5.4) and (5.5) indicate the conditions that govern hourly water release rates. Equation (5.4) can be rearranged to form the following:

$$
\frac{\partial H}{\partial r_t} = p_t \frac{\partial q_t^h}{\partial r_t} + \frac{\partial p_t}{\partial q_t^h} \frac{\partial q_t^h}{\partial r_t} q_t^h \le \frac{\partial c_t^h}{\partial r_t} + \gamma_{t+1} \tag{5.6}
$$

The first part of the right-hand side of equation (5.5) is the marginal benefit of releasing water in period t and can be expressed as the following: $p_t \partial q_t^h / \partial r_t + (\partial p_t / \partial q_t^h)(\partial q_t^h / \partial r_t) q_t^h$. The second part of the right-hand side of equation (5.5) is the marginal cost of releasing water in period t, is given by $\partial c_t^h / \partial r_t + \gamma_{t+1}$ and includes two components. The first part $\partial c_t^h / \partial r_t$ can be thought of as the marginal cost of releasing water and captures the change in operating costs of releasing additional water. The second part γ_{t+1} can be thought of as the shadow price of the water resource constraint and captures the impact that releasing water now has on future net benefits. It can also be thought of as measuring how much the objective function changes when the water release constraint is relaxed by one unit. We include it in the marginal cost component of equations (5.4) to (5.6) since it reflects the opportunity cost of using the water resource to generate hydroelectric power in the current period.

Nevertheless, equations (5.4) and (5.5) are the familiar Kuhn–Tucker necessary conditions for an optimum and can be given the following interpretation. If equation (5.4) is strictly negative and the marginal benefits of releasing water in period t are less than the marginal costs (including the shadow price of the water resource constraint), then equation (5.5) will hold with equality and water releases in that period will be zero. Otherwise, the hydroelectric power dispatcher will release water at a rate up to the point where equation (5.4) holds with equality and will still satisfy equation (5.5). We can take the first part of equation (5.4) and rearrange it into terms more familiar in microeconomics:

$$p_t \frac{\partial q_t^h}{\partial r_t} + \frac{\partial p_t}{\partial q_t^h} \frac{\partial q_t^h}{\partial r_t} q_t^h = p_t \frac{\partial q_t^h}{\partial r_t} (1 + \frac{1}{\eta_t}) \qquad (5.7)$$

where η_t is the familiar elasticity of demand for electricity. Equation (5.7) can be re-expressed as $MR_t(1 + 1/\eta_t)$. This leaves us with a more straightforward interpretation of the first-order conditions that will be familiar to anyone acquainted with standard intermediate and advanced microeconomic theory texts such as Ferguson (1972) and Varian (1992). Upon making this substitution and assuming an interior solution, our first-order condition becomes

$$p_t \frac{\partial q_t^h}{\partial r_t}(1+\frac{1}{\eta_t}) = \frac{\partial c_t^h}{\partial r_t} + \gamma_{t+1} \qquad (5.8)$$

According to this equation, the operator will release water at that rate which equates the marginal benefit of releasing water to the marginal cost of releasing water, taking into account the effects of the equation of motion.

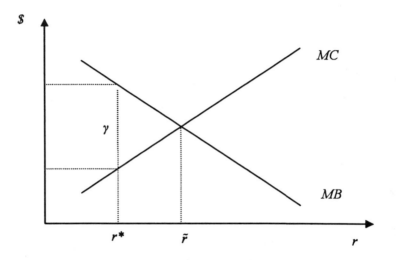

Figure 5.1 Water release rate determination: a graphical view

We can actually present a graphical view of the equation (5.8). In Figure 5.1 above, we measure the water release rate on the horizontal axis and dollars on the vertical axis. Since generation will be a decreasing function of additional water releases (by virtue of our assumption that the production function has a negative second-derivative in the release rate argument), the left–hand side of equation (5.8) will be decreasing in the water release rate argument. In Figure 5.1, we graph this as the downward sloping line labelled MB (Marginal Benefits). If we ignore, for the moment, the shadow price on the right–hand side of equation (5.8), we see that it is increasing in the water release rate argument, by virtue of our assumption that generation costs are increasing (at an increasing rate) in the water release rate argument. As a result, we can represent the right-hand side of equation (5.8) as the upward sloping line labelled MC (Marginal Costs).

If we ignore the water release constraint, water releases would occur at the intersection of the two curves, that is, at $\bar{r}$. However, the operator will incorporate the water resource shadow price, releasing water at a rate given by r^* in Figure 5.1. At r^* the vertical difference between the marginal benefit and marginal cost curves is the shadow price of the water resource.

We can use the above graph to analyse what happens to water releases when there are changes in demand-side or supply-side variables. Higher operating costs, for example, will shift the marginal cost curve to the left (we can think of it as analogous to a decrease in supply in elementary microeconomic theory). As one would imagine, this reduces water release rates. An increase in demand (as would occur during on-peak hours of the day) would shift the marginal benefit curve to the right and result in higher release rates during period t. Figure 5.2 illustrates the example of how an increase in demand changes optimal water release rates.

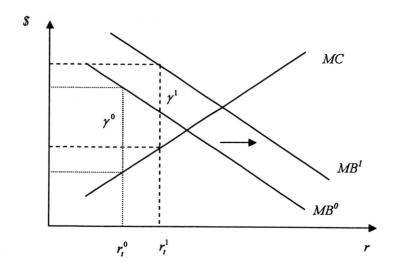

Figure 5.2 How an increase in demand increases water release rates

5.3   DYNAMIC CONDITIONS GOVERNING THE WATER RESOURCE

In the previous chapter, we distinguished between the flow value of water (the direct contribution that releasing water in the current period makes to hydroelectricity generation in the current period) and the stock value of water (the contribution that the stock of water contained in the reservoir makes to the head of the dam). In any given period, the stock value of the water will reflect its value in increasing the generating efficiency of future releases, via effects that storing water has on the head of the dam. Higher release rates in the current period reduce the potential future reservoir elevation, but increase hydroelectric power generation in the current period. In deciding how much water to release in the current period, the hydro dispatcher must weigh the benefits of additional current generation against the potential for reduced future hydroelectricity generating efficiency, particularly when inflows in later periods are insufficient to offset reductions in reservoir elevations caused by water releases in previous periods.

For a given reservoir size, releasing water in the current period increases revenue by $p_t\{\partial q_t^h(r_t, W_t)/\partial r_t\}$ and costs the hydroelectric power dispatcher $\partial c_t^h/\partial r_t$. The net impact of releasing water in the current period is $p_t\{\partial q_t^h(r_t, W_t)/\partial r_t\} - \partial c_t^h/\partial r_t$. However, direct water release costs are invariant with respect to reservoir elevations, so additional water in the reservoir provides additional generation without incurring higher operating expenses. Nevertheless, the dynamic conditions governing the change in the marginal cost of water are embodied in equation (5.9) below, which was obtained by differentiating equation (5.3) with respect to the reservoir content:

$$\frac{\partial H}{\partial W_t} = p_t \frac{\partial q_t^h}{\partial W_t} + \frac{\partial p_t}{\partial q_t^h} \frac{\partial q_t^h}{\partial W_t} q_t^h + \gamma_{t+1} - \gamma_t = 0 \qquad (5.9)$$

We can use the above result involving the elasticity of demand to restate equation (5.9) as:

$$p_t \frac{\partial q_t^h}{\partial W_t}(1+\frac{1}{\eta}) = \gamma_{t+1} - \gamma_t = 0 \qquad (5.10)$$

which we can give the following interpretation. The $p_t(\partial q_t^h/\partial W_t)(1+1/\eta)$ term represents the marginal benefit of additional water, as manifested in higher dam head, when measured in terms of the value of additional hydroelectric power generation for a given rate of water release. The second term in equation (5.10), $\gamma_{t+1} - \gamma_t$, represents the change in the shadow value of the water and reflects the net contribution of the water in future periods. Equation (5.10) can be rearranged as a difference equation (for $\Delta\gamma = \gamma_{t+1} - \gamma_t$) and solved to express the current-period shadow value of water in terms of the value that the stored water has on remaining future period revenues, less the cost of the additional hydroelectricity generation in these periods:

$$\tilde{\gamma}_t = \sum_{t=1}^{T-1} p_t \frac{\partial q_t^h}{\partial W_t}(1+\frac{1}{\eta_t}) + p_T \frac{\partial q_T^h}{\partial W_T}(1+\frac{1}{\eta_T}) \qquad (5.11)$$

Over time, the benefits of storing water will decrease. In the last period, water has value only for its generating value in that period. We also see that γ_t is the sum of these benefits for the remaining periods which decline as we approach the end of the time horizon.

5.4   SIMULATION EXAMPLE

We now present a simulation example of a simple version of the above model. We conduct the simulation using the solver in Microsoft Excel. We will also describe how the simulation was set up so that readers can develop their own models of hydroelectricity generation and conduct their own simulations. In order to implement the simulation, we will make a number of simplifying assumptions. First, we will run the simulation for 24 periods (hours). We will also assume that spot electricity prices are determined exogenously and vary over the course of the simulation. We can easily think of the 24 periods as hours and so we can easily imagine that our 'day' is characterized by periods of lower demand (and hence lower spot prices) and periods of higher demand (and hence higher spot prices). The prices will be expressed in terms of dollars per megawatt and will follow the time path given in Figure 5.3.

According to Figure 5.3, prices are low during the early and late hours of the day. We can easily think of these as off-peak hours. As the hours progress, however, prices rise until they reach their highest point sometime during the middle of the day. We easily think of these as on-peak hours. We will also assume that generating hydroelectric power costs a constant $15 per megawatt to generate. In making this assumption, we also depart from the assumptions in our theoretical model, namely, we assume for the simulation that generation costs are characterized by constant marginal costs and are expressed in terms of costs per unit of generation rather than costs per unit of water release.

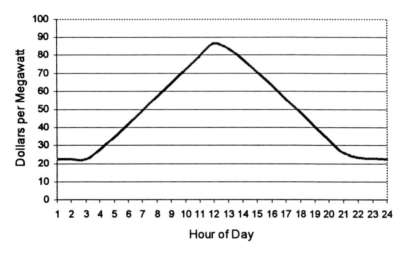

Figure 5.3 Hypothetical spot electricity prices for simulation

In terms of the reservoir, we assume that the reservoir begins with 120000 acre-feet of content. In terms of hydrology, we assume that hourly inflows fluctuate randomly at a rate between 200 and 800 CFS. Generation will occur according to a production of the following form:

$$q_t^h = 0.0005 r_t h_t \qquad (5.12)$$

and we will also assume that dam head depends on content, given by

$$h_t = 0.002 W_t \qquad (5.13)$$

This represents somewhat of a departure from our specification presented in this chapter, but is a little closer to that presented in Chapter 4, where we explicitly define separate functions for head, elevation and content. Please note that we assume that dam head is a linear function of reservoir content. Putting these pieces together yields the following equation for net receipts in period t:

$$\pi_t = (p_t - c_t^q) q_t^h (r_t, H_t(W_t)) \qquad (5.14)$$

where the variable c_t^q represents hydroelectric power generation and transmission costs expressed in dollars per megawatt of generation. Finally, we assume that the operator must release a total of 2000 acre-feet of water during the 24-hour period. The operator will choose rates of water release in each of the 24 periods to maximize the sum of net receipts subject to the equation of motion. For our simulation, we will use a discount rate of 5 per cent (0.05). Finally, we will assume generator capacity limits hourly release rates to 1500 CFS (a small dam). We are now ready to discuss how to solve this model using Microsoft Excel.

5.5   SOLVING THE SIMULATION

Microsoft included a valuable tool in their Excel spreadsheet program. This tool allows one to set up numerical simulation programs and solve them. We will illustrate many of the concepts presented in this book with simulations solved with Microsoft Excel. In order to conduct a simulation, you first need to organize your model and data on a spreadsheet. Table 5.1 is the spreadsheet used to solve this model. We can think of this spreadsheet as consisting of three blocks.

The first block is the basic model parameter block and covers the cells A1 to C6. This block contains the assumptions about the initial reservoir level (cell C2), the discount rate and discount factor (cells C3 and C4) and the production function parameter (cells C5 and C6).

The second block is the operating restriction block and covers cells E1 to H11. This block contains the operating restrictions and behaviour parameters. This block contains the assumption about hydroelectric generation and transmission costs (cells E2 to H2), the inflow minimum and maximum rates (cells E3 to H4), the minimum and maximum release rate assumptions (cells E5 to H6), the value of the objective function which is calculated during the simulation (cells E7 to H7), the total water release constraint and the total amount of water released during the simulation (cells E8 to H9), total inflows into the reservoir calculated during the simulation (cells E10 to H10) and the change in reservoir content calculated during the simulation (cells E11 to H11).

The third block is the model simulation block. This block extends from cells A13 to I38. This part of the spreadsheet is where the simulations are actually performed. Conducting the simulation in Excel is fairly straightforward. Once you have installed the solver (the solver is one of a number of add-ins included with Excel), you lay out the spreadsheet (presumably as I have in Table 5.1). Some of the cells in the model simulation block are formulas. For example, cell B14 contains the starting value for the reservoir content (which it reads from cell C2 and multiplies by 1000). Cells below this cell (cells B15 to B38) are based on a spreadsheet version of the equation of motion. For example, cell B15, which represents the first-period reservoir content, is based on taking the initial content (from cell B14), adding net inflows (inflows minus releases), converting the net inflows figure from CFS to acre-feet and then returns the updated value for reservoir content in the first period. CFS is converted to acre-feet per hour using the following transformation. First, multiply the net inflows by 3600 (this converts seconds to hours). Second, divide the total by 43560 (there are approximately 43 560 cubic feet of water in an acre-foot of water). Finally, add this to the previous period's content to get the current period content. The formula in B15 reads =B14+(C14−D14)*3600/43560. Note that I am placing the operation = in front of every formula. This tells Excel to read the rest of the entry as a formula (and not as a text entry). Cell C14 contains inflows for this period and cell D14 contains releases determined in the simulation.

The next column contains inflows. In this simulation, inflows are determined by Excel's random number generator. If we go back to cells H3 and H4, we have the upper and lower limits on inflows. Using the Excel function RANDBETWEEN, we can generate random inflows between these two bounds (in this case, between 200 and 800 CFS). The entry for cell B14 is =RANDBETWEEN($H$3,$H$4).

The next column contains the release rates determined by the simulation. When you invoke the solver in Excel, you will be prompted to enter a range of cells in the section of the dialogue box entitled By Changing Cells. For our simulation, you would enter $D$15:$D$38. This tells the solver that these are the numbers that will be changed during the simulation to arrive at the value of the objective function that will be maximized.

The next column contains the formula for the head of the dam. It is based on equation (5.13). For cell E14, the formula is =0.002*B14. This column will be updated during each step in the simulation.

The next column contains the formula for generation. It is based on equation (5.12). For cell F14, the formula is =$C$6*D14*E14. This formula takes the production parameter from cell C6 and then multiplies it by the product of release (cell D14) and head (cell E14). This column is also updated during each step in the simulation.

The next column contains the formula for net receipts. It is based on equation (5.14). For cell G14, the formula is =($C$4^A14)*(H14-$H$2)*F14. The first set of parentheses calculates the discount factor. The $C$4 term takes the discount rate (from cell C3) and calculates $1/(1+i)$, where i is the discount rate. The A4 term is just the time period. This becomes the exponent in calculating $1/(1+i)^t$. This term is multiplied by net per-period receipts, which is obtained by taking the difference between the spot price and generation and transmission costs per megawatt (cell H14 minus cell H2) and multiplying the result by generation (cell F14).

The next column contains the spot price for each period. The final column contains the generating efficiency, which is calculated by dividing generation by release, that is, by dividing cell F14 by cell D14.

Table 5.1 Simulation spreadsheet for simple hydroelectric power generation model

	A	B	C	D	E	F	G	H	I
1	Parameters		Values		Operating Restrictions			Values	
2	W Begin		120.00		Hydro G&T Cost			15	
3	δ=		0.05		Inflow Min			200	
4	ρ=		0.95		Inflow Max			800	
5	λ=		2000		Min Release Rate			0	
6	1/λ=		0.0005		Max Release Rate			1 500	
7					Value of Objective Function			60 115	
8					Water Release Requirement			2 000	
9					Total Water Released			2 000	
10					Total Inflows			1 024	
11					Change in Content			-976	
12									
13	t	Content	Inflows	Release	Head	Gen	Net Rev	Price	Gen Eff
14	0	120 000	779	0	240	0.00	0	23	NA
15	1	120 064	628	147	240	17.62	126	23	0.1201
16	2	120 104	493	145	240	17.43	119	23	0.1201
17	3	120 133	429	145	240	17.43	113	23	0.1201
18	4	120 156	775	802	240	96.31	1 010	28	0.1202
19	5	120 154	714	999	240	120.05	1 841	35	0.1202
20	6	120 131	310	1 158	240	139.10	2 789	42	0.1201
21	7	120 061	268	1 249	240	149.93	3 656	49	0.1201
22	8	119 979	510	1 390	240	166.74	4 717	57	0.1200
23	9	119 907	740	1 500	240	179.85	5 714	64	0.1199
24	10	119 844	650	1 500	240	179.76	6 267	72	0.1198
25	11	119 774	313	1 500	240	179.65	6 753	79	0.1198
26	12	119 676	411	1 500	239	179.51	7 175	87	0.1197

Table 5.1 Simulation spreadsheet for simple hydroelectric power generation model (continued)

27	13	119 586	331	1 500	239	179.37	6 543	84	0.1196
28	14	119 489	358	1 500	239	179.22	5 670	78	0.1195
29	15	119 395	442	1 500	239	179.08	4 784	71	0.1194
30	16	119 307	408	1 500	239	178.95	3 948	63	0.1193
31	17	119 217	235	1 441	238	171.73	3 049	56	0.1192
32	18	119 117	420	1 274	238	151.81	2 095	48	0.1191
33	19	119 047	684	1 216	238	144.72	1 473	41	0.1190
34	20	119 003	436	999	238	118.90	816	33	0.1190
35	21	118 956	761	802	238	95.35	367	26	0.1190
36	22	118 953	642	145	238	17.25	50	23	0.1190
37	23	118 994	767	145	238	17.26	44	23	0.1190
38	24	119 045	725	145	238	17.28	41	23	0.1190

We are almost done (simulation examples presented in later chapters will not be described in such detail). All we really need to do now is tell Excel two things. We first have to tell Excel what the objective function is. The objective function is the sum of cells G15 to G38. We have entered this range in cell H7 of the operating restriction block. Second, we have to tell Excel about the constraints.

First, when we invoke the solver, we enter the 'Target Cell' in the solver dialogue box. In our model, this is cell H7 (which contains the formula =SUM(G15:G38)). We also tell Excel that we are maximizing the value of our objective function, so we select the 'Max' option in the 'Equal To' portion of the dialogue box. We then tell Excel that the simulation will be conducted by changing the water release rates and so we enter \$D\$15:\$D\$38 in the 'By Changing Cells' part of the dialogue box. The final part of the dialogue box contains the constraints. The first constraint is that the release rates are greater than zero. To include this, we add the constraint \$D\$15:\$D\$38>=0. We then add the constraint that limits release rates (because of the generator capacity) by adding the constraint \$D\$15:\$D\$38<=\$H\$6. Recall, the cell \$H\$6 contains the maximum release rate. Next, we add the total release requirement. Cell H9 sums the water release rates (in CFS) and converts them to acre-feet. The entry in this cell is =SUM(D15:D38)*3600/43560. Cell C8 contains the total water release requirement of 2000 acre-feet. So the total release constraint will read \$H\$9=\$H\$8. To play it safe, we added an additional constraint to ensure that we never completely drain the reservoir. With the other constraints, we should not really have to add this constraint, but we do so anyway. This constraint reads \$B\$15:\$B\$38>=0.

We are finally ready to solve the model. All we have to do now is click on the 'Solve' command in the dialogue box and the model runs. If we have done everything correctly, the model will iterate towards a solution and will finish, telling us that an optimal solution has been found. The cells in the spreadsheet will automatically be updated with the values selected by the model.

We can take the results of the simulation and graph them. Figure 5.4 shows hourly release rates and generation in each of the 24 hours. Since generation and transmission costs are constant throughout the day, but spot prices rise during the on-peak hours, it should come as no surprise that release rates (and generation) follow the pattern displayed by prices. This behaviour is usually called load-following which means that generation follows demand. This behaviour illustrates behaviour that has been termed hydro-shifting, which refers to storing water behind the dam during off-peak hours and releasing the water for generation during on-peak hours. This phenomenon is described in Edwards et al. (1992) and in Edwards et al. (1999).

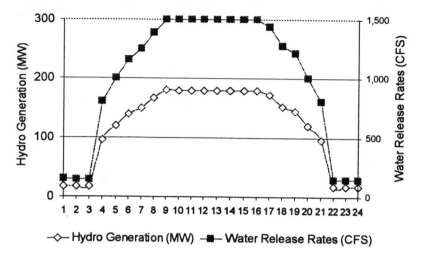

Figure 5.4 Water releases and hydroelectric power generation

One issue that we have discussed in earlier chapters, and will be discussed in later chapters, is the effect the changes in head have on generating efficiency. The last column of the spreadsheet contains the generating efficiency figures from the simulation. While they do not change by very much over the course of the day (we are only releasing 2000 acre-feet of water), they do decline as the content of the reservoir falls. For example, when reservoir content is 120 064 acre-feet in the first period, the generating efficiency is 0.1201. As water is released, and as reservoir content drops, we see the generating efficiency drop as well. By the end of the day, the content has dropped to 119 045 and the generating efficiency has dropped to 0.1190. This 0.85 per cent reduction in reservoir content caused a 0.91 per cent reduction in generating efficiency. This is precisely the head effect that we referred to in earlier chapters. What is not clear from this example, of course, is whether this head effect had any bearing on the pattern of water releases over the course of the day. In later chapters, we will introduce more complete models that show more pronounced head effects that likely influence how water is released over the course of the day.

5.6   HYDROELECTRIC POWER PROVISION WITH THERMAL INTEGRATION

Many hydroelectricity generating facilities supplement hydroelectric power with other power, either generated by thermal facilities that they either own or operate, or through power purchased for resale. This is often the case with the Power Marketing Administrations in the United States that are contractually bound to meet contract commitments to their so-called firm power customers. We can easily modify the above model to incorporate either thermal generation or purchases for resale. In this section, we consider the first case, namely, where the hydroelectric dispatcher operates thermal generating facilities used to supplement their generation of hydroelectric power. To incorporate this possibility, the objective function is modified in two ways. First, the total power sold by the dispatcher will be the sum of hydroelectric power and thermal power, instead of depending on just hydroelectric power alone. Second, costs for thermal generation are $c_t^t(q_t^t)$, where q_t^t refers to thermal generation in period t. As with the cost function for hydroelectric power generation, we assume that this function is twice–continuously differentiable and has positive first– and second–derivatives. Thermal generation will be constrained by the capacity of the thermal generator, a constraint that we will specify as $q_t^t \leq \bar{q}^t$, where $\bar{q}^t$ represents the capacity of the thermal generating unit. With these two modifications, the single-period objective function becomes:

$$\pi_t = p_t(Q_t)[q_t^h(r_t, H_t(W_t)) + q_t^t] - c_t^h(r_t) - c_t^t(q_t^t) \qquad (5.15)$$

Under the assumption that the hydroelectric power dispatcher supplements hydroelectricity generation with thermal generation, the dispatcher will choose rates of water release and thermal generation in each period to maximize the sum of net receipts over the T-period time horizon subject to the same equation of motion used in the previous problem and the capacity constraint on thermal generation. The resulting Hamiltonian function is then:

$$H = \sum_{t=1}^{T-1} \{ p_t(Q_t)[q_t^h(r_t, W_t) + q_t^l] - c_t^h(r_t) - c_t^l(q_t^l)$$
$$+ \gamma_{t+1}(W_{t+1} - W_t + r_t - f_t) + \mu_t(\overline{q}^l - q_t^l)\} \qquad (5.16)$$
$$+ p_T(Q_T)[q_T^h(r_T, W_T) + q_T^l] - c_T^h(r_T) - c_T^l(q_T^l)$$
$$+ \gamma_T(W_T + r_T - f_T) + \mu_T(\overline{q}^l - q_T^l)$$

Maximizing this equation with respect to the water release rate yields the same Kuhn–Tucker first–order conditions as in the last problem (as given in equations 5.4 to 5.6 and subject to the same interpretation). Maximizing this equation with respect to the thermal generation control variable yields the following Kuhn-Tucker first-order conditions on thermal generation:

$$\frac{\partial H}{\partial q_t^l} = p_t + \frac{\partial p_t}{\partial q_t^l} q_t^l - \frac{\partial c_t^l}{\partial q_t^l} - \mu_t \leq 0 \qquad (5.17)$$

$$q_t^l \frac{\partial H}{\partial q_t^l} = 0 \qquad (5.18)$$

These first-order conditions can be interpreted in a fashion analogous to the first-order conditions on water releases in the original problem. Under an interior solution, thermal generation will occur up to the rate at which the marginal benefits equal the marginal costs. Under an interior solution, equations (5.17) and (5.18) can be combined to form the following:

$$\frac{\partial H}{\partial q_t^l} = p_t(1 + \frac{1}{\eta_t}) = \frac{\partial c_t^l}{\partial q_t^l} + \mu_t \qquad (5.19)$$

We can combine the first-order conditions on thermal generation with those for hydroelectric power generation to form the following ratio of marginal revenues to marginal costs:

$$\frac{\partial q_t^h}{\partial r_t} = \frac{\dfrac{\partial c_t^h}{\partial r_t} + \gamma_{t+1}}{\dfrac{\partial c_t^h}{\partial q_t^t} + \mu_t} \tag{5.20}$$

Equation (5.20) is obtained by dividing (5.9) by equation (5.19). This condition is analogous to the condition that the marginal rate of transformation equal the ratio of marginal costs in the neoclassical microeconomic theory of the firm.

5.7   SIMULATING HYDRO-THERMAL INTEGRATION

We now present a simple simulation of hydroelectricity generation with thermal integration. The basic model will be the same as that presented earlier, except we now assume the operator also owns a thermal generator with 75 megawatts of generating capacity. In addition, we assume that thermal generation cost $50 per megawatt (fully-loaded system-wide costs) and faces the same prices as in the previous simulation. The spreadsheet differs from the original in two important respects. First, we add a column to include thermal generation, which is now a decision variable (along with water releases). Second, we add an operating constraint that limits thermal generation to its rated maximum of 75 megawatts. The objective function changes slightly to include net receipts from thermal generation. The results of this simulation are presented in Figure 5.5 and Table 5.2.

In this simulation, the pattern of water releases, and hence hydroelectricity generation, is essentially unchanged from the previous example. Once prices rise to exceed the costs of thermal generation, thermal generation remains constant through most of the day. In this manner, the operator can easily integrate hydroelectric power generation with thermal power generation to meet customer load.

Table 5.2 Simulation spreadsheet for hydroelectric--thermal generation

	A	B	C	D	E	F	G	H	I	J
1	Parameters	Value			Operating Restrictions					
2	W Beg	120.0			Hydro G&T Cost = 15					
3	δ=	0.05			Thermal G&T Cost= 50					
4	ρ=	0.95			Inflow Min= 200					
5	λ=	2000			Inflow Max= 800					
6	1/λ=	0.0005			Min Release Rate= 0					
7					Max Release Rate = 1500					
8					Thermal Gen Capacity = 75					
9					Value of Objective Function = 70,273					
10					Water Release Requirement = 2,000					
11					Total Water Released = 2,000					
12					Total Inflows= 978					
13					Change in Content= -1,022					
14	t	Cont (000 AF)	In-flow	Rel	Ther Gen.	Head	Gen.	Net Rev	Price	Gen Eff
15	0	120.0	750	338	0	240	41	304	23	0.120
16	1	120.0	522	635	0	240	76	544	22	0.120
17	2	120.0	231	635	0	240	76	518	22	0.120
18	3	120.0	581	635	0	240	76	493	22	0.120
19	4	120.0	200	714	0	240	86	898	28	0.120
20	5	119.9	501	816	75	240	98	595	35	0.120
21	6	119.9	425	926	75	240	111	1,770	42	0.120
22	7	119.9	263	1,037	75	240	124	2,993	49	0.120
23	8	119.8	588	1,149	75	240	138	4,238	57	0.120
24	9	119.8	483	1,262	75	240	151	5,489	64	0.120
25	10	119.7	538	1,374	75	239	165	6,734	72	0.120
26	11	119.6	451	1,487	75	239	178	7,965	79	0.120
27	12	119.5	666	1,500	75	239	179	8,699	87	0.120
28	13	119.5	708	1,500	75	239	179	7,876	84	0.120
29	14	119.4	301	1,462	75	239	175	6,566	78	0.119
30	15	119.3	746	1,356	75	239	162	5,059	71	0.119
31	16	119.3	670	1,245	75	239	149	3,726	63	0.119
32	17	119.2	361	1,133	75	238	135	2,583	56	0.119
33	18	119.2	602	1,021	75	238	122	1,621	48	0.119
34	19	119.1	547	908	75	238	108	825	41	0.119
35	20	119.1	262	796	75	238	95	176	33	0.119
36	21	119.0	440	683	0	238	81	312	26	0.119
37	22	119.0	659	650	0	238	77	223	23	0.119
38	23	119.0	560	639	0	238	76	193	23	0.119
39	24	119.0	527	636	0	238	76	178	23	0.119

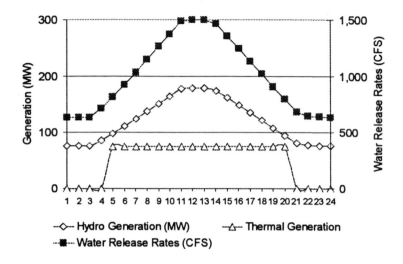

Figure 5.5 Hydroelectric and thermal generation simulation results

5.8   INTEGRATING ENVIRONMENTAL IMPACTS: A SIMPLE EXAMPLE

If we return to the first model presented in this chapter (without thermal integration), we can illustrate how one might integrate environmental or ecological impacts into water release decisions. Admittedly, the approach will be far too simplistic to be applicable to a very wide range of environmental or ecological issues, so it is presented for illustrative purposes only. Let us begin by specifying a naive damage function of the form:

$$D_t = D_r(r_t) \qquad (5.21)$$

For the sake of simplicity, we imagine this damage function to be decreasing for low rates of water release (we need to release at least some minimum amount of water to support downstream habitats). As we release more water from the dam, damages fall. However, we eventually reach a point, for example $\underline{r}$, where water release rates become so high as to cause other forms of environmental or ecological damage, so beyond a certain rate of water release, damage increases. Figure 5.6 illustrates such a naive version of this damage function.

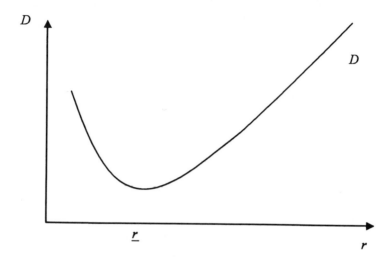

Figure 5.6 Naive damage function example

We could easily come up with a more complicated damage function, perhaps one that relates damage to fluctuations in, rather than levels of, water release rates. Moreover, we are basing damage solely on flow rates. We could even imagine a specification of environmental quality in a more complex dynamic form, where a given stock of environmental quality is affected by water release rates or fluctuations in water release rates. We also have to keep in mind that every downstream environment will have a different physical and ecological make-up, so we must not fool ourselves into thinking that we can encompass a very broad range of downstream impacts with such a simple function.

These caveats aside, if we add equation (5.21) to our original problem, we obtain the following Hamiltonian function:

$$\sum_{t=1}^{T-1} \{ p_t(Q_t) q_t^h(r_t, W_t) - c_t^h(r_t) - D_t(r_t)$$

$$+ \gamma_{t+1}(W_{t+1} - W_t + r_t - f_t) \} \tag{5.22}$$

$$+ p_T(Q_T) q_T^h(r_T, W_T) - c_T^h(r_T) - D_T(r_T)$$

$$+ \gamma_T(W_T + r_T - f_T)$$

Under an interior solution, the first-order conditions on water release rates are given by the following:

$$p_t \frac{\partial q_t^h}{\partial r_t}(1 + \frac{1}{\eta_t}) = \frac{\partial c_t^h}{\partial r_t} + \frac{\partial D_t}{\partial r_t} + \gamma_{t+1} \tag{5.23}$$

According to this equation, the operator will release water at that rate which equates the marginal benefit of releasing water to the marginal cost of releasing water, taking into account the marginal damages, given by the $\partial D_t / \partial r_t$ term on the right-hand side of equation (5.23) and the equation of motion. Given our naive specification of damages, marginal damages are negative for low rates of water release and are positive for water release rates above r. If we confine water releases in our example to a range where marginal damages are positive, we can modify Figure 5.7 to incorporate damages to determine a new optimal rate of water release. In Figure 5.1, the curve labelled MC* includes marginal damages (and can be thought of as the sum of private marginal release costs and marginal damages). Under these assumptions, the optimal rate of water release falls from the original r^* to the new r^{**}. If we included the full range of marginal damages, we would not only have a more complicated figure to decipher, but we would also run into situations where incorporating damages into the decision could cause water release rates to *increase*, rather than decrease as they did in our example.

Again, this example represents a special case of a model derived from a naive damage function, so its applicability may be limited. On the other hand, it does illustrate how one might develop a more sophisticated and realistic model that incorporates impacts of water releases on the downstream environment. If one were to develop a more sophisticated model of damage, there are three factors than one might wish to incorporate. The first factor is the rate of water releases. The naive damage function that we presented above is but one example of how to specify a relationship between damage and water release rates. The second factor is the variability in water release rates. For example, a damage function that depended on the mean and standard deviation (or variance) of water release rates might be one way to capture the impacts of these first two factors. The third factor could be the existing state of the downstream environment. This is somewhat trickier to incorporate since you are now leaving the realm of simpler static relationships between releases and damage and entering the realm of potentially a more complex dynamic relationship between a flow in water to a stock representing a given state of nature that will change with changes in downstream flows. In some cases, flooding can actually improve the downstream environment, as evidenced by interest in mimicking spring floods through periodic high rates of water release (Collier et al., 1997), but in other cases could damage the downstream environment.

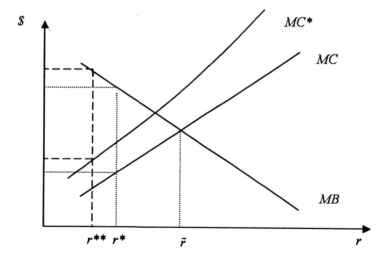

Figure 5.7 Water releases with naive damage function

5.9   SUMMARY AND CONCLUSIONS

This chapter has presented two simple models of hydroelectric power generation. The first model was of an operator that engaged in hydroelectricity generation only. The second model added thermal power generation to the operator's power supply portfolio. We also presented a simulation for each model that showed how time-of-day variations in price influenced the hourly pattern of hydroelectricity generation and, in the case of the second model, thermal power generation. In the models presented in this chapter, the only restriction imposed on the operator was a total release requirement that forced the operator to release a fixed quantity of water over the course of the simulation. Finally, we presented a simple example of a model that incorporates environmental and ecological impacts using a naive damage function. In the next chapter, we will add restrictions that limit the flexibility of the operator in terms of how much water can be released in each period and how much water release rates can be changed between periods.

6. An economic model of hydroelectric power provision with environmental constraints

In this chapter we extend the model presented in the previous chapter to include environmental constraints. These constraints include restrictions on water release rates, ramping restrictions and other restrictions with which dam operators are usually subject to comply.

6.1 THE ENVIRONMENTAL CONSTRAINTS

The model presented in this chapter is essentially the same as presented in the last chapter. What is different about the model presented here is the presence of a series of constraints imposed on the dispatcher that limit the hourly pattern of water releases. The purposes of these environmental constraints are twofold. The first purpose is to limit the amount of damage that can occur to the downstream environment. The second purpose of these constraints is to allow the operation of the hydroelectric power plant and, at the same time, satisfy any other objectives that exist for the water, whether it be uses of the water for municipal water supplies, irrigation or any other purpose. The first constraint that we will impose is a minimum release constraint, that requires the dispatcher to release a minimum amount of water, $\tilde{r}_t$, in each period. Minimum release constraints are usually imposed to ensure adequate downstream flows to protect the indigenous downstream habitat and to meet irrigation and other objectives. We express this constraint as $r_t \geq \tilde{r}_t$. We also impose a constraint that requires the dispatcher to release water at a rate that does not exceed $\bar{r}_t$ in each period. We express this maximum release constraint as $r_t \leq \bar{r}_t$. The third constraint limits the rate at which hourly water release rates can be increased in any given period. We express this ramp-up constraint as $r_t - r_{t-1} \leq r^u$. The fourth constraint limits the rate at which water release rates can decrease in adjacent periods. We express this ramp-down constraint as $r_{t-1} - r_t \leq r^d$. These last two constraints are intended to prevent downstream environmental damage that many believe is caused by sudden changes in water release rates. Our final constraint is that the dispatcher is required to release a fixed amount of water over the entire time horizon. We express this total water release constraint as $R = \sum_{t=1}^{T} r_t$ where R is the quantity of water that must be released over the time horizon (this can be expressed in acre-feet, or any other volumetric measure).

6.1.1   MAXIMIZATION UNDER RESOURCE AND RELEASE CONSTRAINTS

As in our previously discussed models, the dispatcher will choose rates of water release to maximize the discounted present value of profits subject to our usual equation of motion and the above five environmental constraints, namely the minimum and maximum release constraints, the ramp-up and ramp-down constraints and the total water release constraint. Optimizing over T periods yields the following objective function that will be maximized with respect to hourly water release rates, r_t . In this model, we do not assume that the hydroelectric power dispatcher either generates thermal power or purchases thermal power for resale.

Following the conventions established in the previous chapter, we define γ_{t+1} as the discrete-time costate associated with the equation of motion and define the δ's as the shadow prices on the minimum release, maximum release and ramping constraints. We also define γ_T as the final period costate on the equation of motion, and ψ as the costate on the total water release requirement. Our revised objective function is given in equation (6.1).

$$J = \sum_{t=1}^{T-1} \{ p_t (Q_t) q_t^h (r_t , W_t) - c_t^h (r_t)$$

$$- \gamma_{t+1} (W_{t+1} - W_t + r_t - f_t)$$

$$- \tilde{\delta}_t (\tilde{r} - r_t) + \overline{\delta}_t (\overline{r} - r_t)$$

$$+ \delta_t^d (r^u - (r_t - r_{t-1})) + \delta_t^d (r^d - (r_{t-1} - r_t))\}$$

$$+ p_T (Q_T) q_T^h (r_T , W_T) - c_T^h (r_T) \tag{6.1}$$

$$+ \gamma_T (W_T - r_T + f_T) + \psi (R - \sum_{t=1}^{T} r_t)$$

$$- \tilde{\delta}_T (\tilde{r} - r_T) + \overline{\delta}_T (\overline{r} - r_T)$$

$$+ \delta_T^d (r^u - (r_T - r_{T-1})) + \delta_T^d (r^d - (r_{T-1} - r_T))$$

6.1.2 OPTIMIZATION UNDER THE TOTAL WATER RELEASE CONSTRAINT

For expository convenience, we examine how dispatcher behaviour is affected by the constraints sequentially. We first examine dispatcher behaviour under the assumption that only the total water release constraint is binding. We shall introduce the effects of the other environmental constraints later in the chapter. If we apply the Kuhn–Tucker conditions and discrete-time maximum principle to equation (6.1) with respect to water releases, the Kuhn–Tucker conditions on the water releases are:

$$\frac{\partial J}{\partial r_t} = p_t \frac{\partial q_t^h (\cdot)}{\partial r_t} (1 + \frac{1}{\eta_t}) - \frac{\partial c_t^h (\cdot)}{\partial r_t} - \gamma_{t+1} - \psi \leq 0 \tag{6.2}$$

$$r_t \frac{\partial J}{\partial r_t} = r_t [\cdot] = 0 \tag{6.3}$$

As in the previous chapter, η_t is the elasticity of demand in period t and we have already completed the algebraic simplifications to arrive at the first-order conditions in this form. Again, this renders that part of the left-hand side of equation (6.2) analogous to the marginal revenue term common in many profit maximization problems. According to equation (6.2), the power dispatcher will weigh the marginal revenue product of water releases, given by $p_t(\partial q_t^h/\partial r_t)(1+1/\eta_t)$, against the marginal costs of water releases, given by $\partial c_t^h/\partial r_t$. In contrast to previous problems, the dispatcher must now also weigh the shadow prices of the water resource and the total release requirement. In any period, water will be released to generate hydroelectric power as long as the marginal costs of releasing water, including the effect of the water resource and minimum release constraints, are no greater than the marginal revenue of releasing water. In the event of an interior solution, the above equations simplify to:

$$p_t \frac{\partial q_t^h}{\partial r_t}(1+\frac{1}{\eta_t})=\frac{\partial c_t^h}{\partial r_t}+\gamma_{t+1}+\psi \qquad (6.4)$$

The shadow price on the total water release constraint can be given more than one interpretation. On the one hand, a binding total water release constraint represents an upper limit on the amount of water than can be released which, if relaxed, induces more releases from the reservoir. On the other hand, and since the constraint has to be satisfied with equality, it also represents a lower limit on the total amount of water to be released over the time horizon. This interpretation suggests that including the costate variable on the left-hand side of equation (6.4) is appropriate, and the dispatcher is encouraged to bring water release rates up to meet the constraint by the end of the time horizon.

6.1.3 OPTIMIZATION WHEN THE ENVIRONMENTAL CONSTRAINTS ARE BINDING

We consider what happens when the minimum release and total water release constraints are binding. In this case, and again under an interior solution, the Kuhn-Tucker condition on water releases simplifies to the following:

$$p_t \frac{\partial q_t^h}{\partial r_t}(1+\frac{1}{\eta_t}) = \frac{\partial c_t^h}{\partial r_t} + \gamma_{t+1} + \psi - \tilde{\delta}_t \qquad (6.5)$$

When this constraint is binding, additional water must be released to meet this limit, thereby offsetting the potentially negative effects that the water resource and total water release constraints have on per-period water release rates. Such could be the situation during periods of low electricity demand when prices are low, but expected to be higher in later periods of the time horizon. Such a situation could easily occur during off-peak hours (if we interpret each time period in these terms) when demand (and hence price) are low, but expected to increase as system load increases into the on-peak hours.

When the maximum water release constraint is binding, we get the opposite effect. In this case, and under an interior solution, the Kuhn–Tucker condition on water releases is given by:

$$p_t \frac{\partial q_t^h}{\partial r_t}(1+\frac{1}{\eta_t}) = \frac{\partial c_t^h}{\partial r_t} + \gamma_{t+1} + \psi + \overline{\delta}_t \qquad (6.6)$$

When this constraint is binding, water releases must be reduced to meet this constraint, thereby reinforcing the effects of the water resource and total water release constraints. Such could be the situation during periods of high demand when prices are higher, but expected to be lower in later periods of the time horizon. We can easily envision this occurring during on-peak hours of greater demand.

6.1.4   THE IMPACT OF THE RAMPING CONSTRAINTS

According to the above analysis, the effects of the minimum and maximum release constraints are felt directly in the periods in which water is released. For example, a minimum release constraint binding in an off-peak hour (for example, during the middle of the night during late spring or early autumn) effectively forces releases up to the minimum required. Conversely, a binding maximum release constraint (as would be the case during an on-peak hour in the middle of summer) forces water release rates down to the binding maximum. In contrast, the ramping requirements can affect both current-period and next-period water release rates.

In the event that the ramp-up requirement is binding, and under an interior solution, the Kuhn–Tucker condition on water releases is given by:

$$p_t \frac{\partial q_t^h}{\partial r_t}(1+\frac{1}{\eta_t}) = \frac{\partial c_t^h}{\partial r_t} + \gamma_{t+1} + \psi + \delta_t^u - \delta_{t+1}^u \tag{6.7}$$

According to equation (6.7), the ramp-up requirement has opposing effects on current-period water release rates. On the one hand, the current period shadow price on the ramp-up constraint, δ_t^u, discourages water releases in the current period. On the other hand, higher water releases in the current period also make meeting the ramp-up requirement in the next period easier. With a binding next-period ramp-up requirement, as evidenced by its shadow price, δ_{t+1}^u, being greater than zero, water releases can be increased in the current period to offset the effects of a binding ramp-up constraint in the current period.

The opposite result obtains when the ramp-down constraint is binding, as suggested by the following Kuhn–Tucker condition on water releases:

$$p_t \frac{\partial q_t^h}{\partial r_t}(1+\frac{1}{\eta_t}) = \frac{\partial c_t^h}{\partial r_t} + \gamma_{t+1} + \psi - \delta_t^d + \delta_{t+1}^d \tag{6.8}$$

In this instance, the current period shadow price on the ramp-down constraint, δ_t^d, increases water releases in the current period. However, higher water releases in the current period also make meeting the ramp-down requirement in the next period more difficult. A binding next-period ramp-down requirement, as evidenced by its shadow price, δ_{t+1}^d, being greater than zero, indicates that water releases can be reduced in the current period to offset the effects of a binding ramp-down constraint in the current period.

6.2 SIMULATING HYDROELECTRIC GENERATION UNDER ENVIRONMENTAL CONSTRAINTS

Here we present the results of simulating the simple hydro model presented in Chapter 5 with the addition of a series of environmental constraints. The first environmental constraint that we impose is a minimum–release constraint that requires that the operator release at a minimum rate of 250 CFS. Such a constraint might be imposed to guarantee a minimum downstream flow to protect downstream wildlife or downstream recreational activities such as river-rafting or fishing. If we compare the results of the simulation without the minimum release constraint (see Figure 5.4) to that with the minimum release constraint (Figure 6.1), we notice that water releases and hence hydroelectric generation are somewhat smoother with the minimum release constraint. In Figure 6.1, we compare water release rates between the no-constraint simulation and the minimum release constraint simulation.

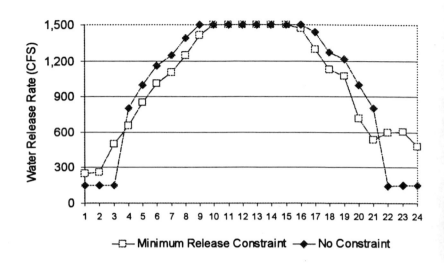

Figure 6.1 Water releases under a minimum release constraint

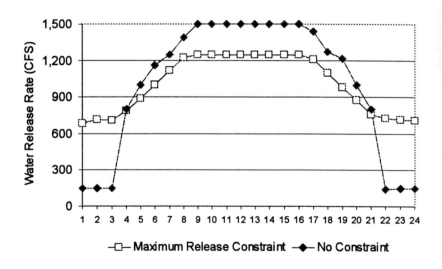

Figure 6.2 Water releases with minimum and maximum release constraints

When we impose a maximum release constraint (that is below the generator capacity), we smooth hourly release rates even further, as indicated in Figure 6.2. In this simulation, we maintain the 250 CFS minimum release constraint of the previous simulation, but also impose a 1250 CFS maximum release rate constraint. In this simulation, release rates reach the constraint during the middle of the day, but also start at a higher rate in the off-peak hours of the day. This smoothing occurs partly due to the binding total release constraint, which has been imposed on all simulations performed thus far.

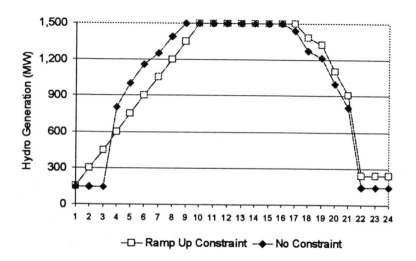

Figure 6.3 Water releases with ramp-up constraint

If we impose a ramp-up constraint that limits the rate at which water releases can increase from one hour to the next to 150 CFS, then we smooth release rates even further, as evidenced by Figure 6.3. We certainly observe release rates meeting the maximum of 1500 CFS (recall that we compare this simulation to the original simulation with no other restrictions), but we reach our generator capacity one hour later in the day than without the ramp-up restriction. It turns out that the ramping restriction is not binding in every hour. When we compare the original simulation to the ramp-up simulation, the no-ramping requirement simulation has ramp-up rates greater than the 150 CFS limit in hours four to six (656 CFS, 198 CFS and 159 CFS, respectively, in those hours).

A closer look at Figure 6.3 also reveals that the ramp-down rates between the two simulations are very similar. Figure 6.4 shows what happens when we add a ramp-down restriction to the original simulation with no environmental restrictions. In this simulation, not only does the operator ramp-down at a much smoother rate, but also ramps-up at a much smoother rate.

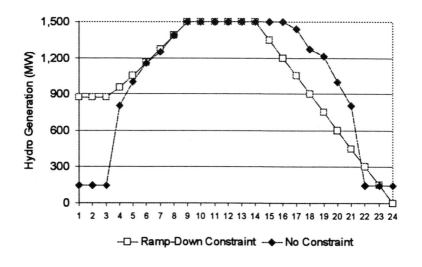

Figure 6.4 Water releases with ramp-down constraint

Figure 6.5 compares a simulation with both ramp-up and ramp-down restrictions to the simulation with no environmental restrictions. While hourly changes in water release rates are smaller (in absolute value) in this simulation than they are in the original simulation with no environmental constraints, hourly ramp-up rates are higher in this simulation than they are under the simulation with the ramp-down restriction only.

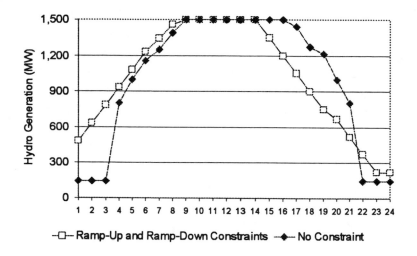

Figure 6.5 Water releases with ramp-up and ramp-down constraints

We finally consider imposing all environmental restrictions simultaneously. Figure 6.6 compares the original simulation with no environmental restrictions to that with all environmental restrictions (minimum and maximum release constraints and ramp-up and ramp-down constraints). As is apparent from this figure, when these restrictions are imposed simultaneously, water release rates are much smoother than under the baseline simulation with no such restrictions. This suggests that the desire to dampen fluctuations in hourly water release rates requires a fairly broad set of environmental restrictions, and that this set of environmental restrictions be imposed simultaneously.

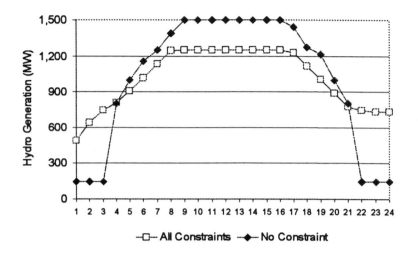

Figure 6.6 Water release rates with all environmental restrictions

6.3   HYDROELECTRIC POWER PROVISION WITH THERMAL INTEGRATION

Many hydroelectricity generating facilities supplement hydroelectric power with other power, either generated by thermal facilities that they own or operate, or through power purchased for resale. This is often the case with the Power Marketing Administrations in the United States that are contractually bound to meet contract commitments to their so-called firm power customers. We shall take a closer look at the operations of a Power Marketing Administration in the next chapter. For now, we can easily modify our model to incorporate either thermal power generation or purchases for resale to capture releasing water and generating thermal electricity (or purchasing power for resale) simultaneously. In this section, we extend our model with environmental constraints to include the possibility that the hydroelectric power dispatcher can supplement their power provision by operating thermal power generating facilities. To incorporate this possibility, the objective function is modified in two ways. First, the total power sold by the dispatcher will be the sum of hydroelectric power and thermal power, instead of depending on just hydroelectric power alone. Second, costs for thermal generation are $c_t^t(q_t^t)$, where q_t^t refers to thermal power generation in period t. As with the cost function for hydroelectric power generation, we assume that this function is twice continuously differentiable and has positive first- and second–derivatives. Thermal generation will be constrained by the capacity of the thermal generator, a constraint that we will specify as $q_t^t \leq \overline{q}^t$, where $\overline{q}^t$ represents the capacity of the thermal generating unit. With these two modifications, the single-period objective function becomes:

$$\pi_t = p_t(Q_t)[q_t^h(r_t, W_t) + q_t^t] - c_t^h(r_t) - c_t^t(q_t^t) \tag{6.9}$$

Under the assumption that the hydroelectric power dispatcher supplements hydroelectric generation with thermal power generation, the T-period optimization problem becomes the following:

$$
\begin{aligned}
J = \sum_{t=1}^{T-1} & \{ p_t(Q_t)[q_t^h(r_t, W_t) + q_t^t] - c_t^h(r_t) - c_t^t(q_t^t) \\
& - \gamma_{t+1}(W_{t+1} - W_t + r_t - f_t) - \tilde{\delta}_t(\tilde{r} - r_t) + \overline{\delta}_t(\overline{r} - r_t) \\
& + \delta_t^d(r^u - (r_t - r_{t-1})) + \delta_t^d(r^d - (r_{t-1} - r_t)) + \phi_t^t(\overline{q}^t - q_t^t) \} \\
& + p_T(Q_T)[q_T^h(r_T, W_T) + q_T^t] - c_T^h(r_T) - c_T^t(q_T^t) \\
& + \gamma_T(W_T - r_T + f_T) + \psi(R - \sum_{t=1}^T r_t) - \tilde{\delta}_T(\tilde{r} - r_T) \\
& + \overline{\delta}_T(\overline{r} - r_T) + \delta_T^d(r^u - (r_T - r_{T-1})) \\
& + \delta_T^d(r^d - (r_{T-1} - r_T)) + \phi_T^t(\overline{q}^t - q_T^t)
\end{aligned}
\tag{6.10}
$$

In the above equation, we represent the shadow price of the thermal generating capacity constraint as ϕ_t^t. Since the first-order conditions on the water release variable remain unchanged from the previous example, we focus on the first-order conditions on thermal power generation, which become the following:

$$\frac{\partial J}{\partial q_t^i} = p_t(1+\frac{1}{\eta_t}) - \frac{\partial c_t^i}{\partial q_t^i} - \phi_t \leq 0 \qquad (6.11)$$

$$q_t^i \frac{\partial J}{\partial q_t^i} = q_t^i [\cdot] = 0 \qquad (6.12)$$

Equations (6.11) and (6.12) have an analogous interpretation to the first-order conditions on water releases given in equations (6.2) and (6.3) above. Accordingly, the hydroelectric power dispatcher will generate thermal power up to the point where the marginal revenue from additional thermal power generation just equals the marginal cost of thermal power generation, including the shadow price of the thermal generating capacity constraint.

6.3.1   HYDRO-THERMAL INTEGRATION IN THE ABSENCE OF ENVIRONMENTAL CONSTRAINTS

In the event that the minimum release constraint is not binding, but thermal power generation is combined with hydroelectricity generation, as would occur under an interior solution, equations (6.4), (6.11) and (6.12) can be combined to form the following equation:

$$\frac{\partial q_t^h}{\partial r_t} = \frac{\frac{\partial c_t^h}{\partial r_t} + \gamma_{t+1} + \psi}{\frac{\partial c_t^i}{\partial q_t^i} + \phi_t^i} \qquad (6.13)$$

Equation (6.13) indicates the conditions under which hydroelectric power generation will be combined with thermal power generation. The dispatcher will combine hydroelectric with thermal power generation in that combination that equates the ratio of the marginal products of hydroelectric and thermal generation to the ratio of the marginal costs of each. Of course, this condition is analogous to equating the marginal rate of transformation to the ratio of the marginal costs from neoclassical production theory.

6.3.2 HYDRO-THERMAL INTEGRATION WITH ENVIRONMENTAL CONSTRAINTS

In the event that the minimum release constraint is binding, equation (6.13) is modified to become:

$$\frac{\partial q_t^h(\cdot)}{\partial r_t} = \frac{\dfrac{\partial c_t^h(\cdot)}{\partial r_t} + \gamma_{t+1} + \psi - \tilde{\delta}_t}{\dfrac{\partial c_t^t(\cdot)}{\partial q_t^t} + \phi_t^t} \qquad (6.14)$$

According to this equation, a binding minimum release constraint reduces the marginal cost of hydroelectric power generation (including the shadow prices on the water resource and minimum release constraint) by offsetting the effects of the water resource and total water release constraints. For a given rate of water release, the hydroelectric power dispatcher will reduce thermal power generation accordingly to maintain equality between the marginal product of hydroelectric power generation and the ratio of the marginal generation costs.

A binding maximum release requirement has the opposite effect, as indicated by equation (6.15):

$$\frac{\partial q_t^h(\cdot)}{\partial r_t} = \frac{\dfrac{\partial c_t^h(\cdot)}{\partial r_t} + \gamma_{t+1} + \psi + \bar{\delta}_t}{\dfrac{\partial c_t^t(\cdot)}{\partial q_t^t} + \phi_t^t} \qquad (6.15)$$

According to this equation, a binding maximum release constraint increases the marginal cost of hydroelectricity generation (including the shadow prices on the water resource and maximum release constraint) by adding to the effects of the water resource and total water release constraints. For a given rate of water release, the hydroelectric power dispatcher will increase thermal power generation accordingly to maintain equality between the marginal product of hydroelectricity generation and the ratio of the marginal generation costs.

As in the case without the environmental constraints, the minimum and maximum release constraints are felt directly in the periods in which water is released. For example, a minimum release constraint binding in an off-peak hour (for example, during the middle of the night during late spring or early autumn) effectively forces releases up to the minimum required. Conversely, a binding maximum release constraint (as would be the case during an on-peak hour in the middle of summer) forces water release rates down to the binding maximum. As in the case of no thermal integration, the ramping requirements can affect both current-period and next-period water release rates. In the event that the ramp-up requirement is binding and under an interior solution, the Kuhn–Tucker conditions on water releases and thermal generation can be arranged to yield:

$$\frac{\partial q_t^h}{\partial r_t} = \frac{\dfrac{\partial c_t^h}{\partial r_t} + \gamma_{t+1} + \psi + \delta_t^u - \delta_{t+1}^u}{\dfrac{\partial c_t'(\cdot)}{\partial q_t'} + \phi_t'} \tag{6.16}$$

According to equation (6.16), the ramp-up requirement has opposing effects on current-period water release rates. On the one hand, the current period shadow price on the ramp-up constraint, δ_t^u, discourages water releases in the current period. On the other hand, higher water releases in the current period also make meeting the ramp-up requirement in the next period easier. A binding next-period ramp-up requirement, as evidenced by its shadow price, δ_{t+1}^u, being greater than zero, indicates that water releases can be increased in the current period to offset the effects of a binding ramp-up constraint in the current period. Such a situation could lead to higher thermal generation in the current period followed by lower thermal generation in the next period.

The opposite result obtains when the ramp-down constraint is binding, as suggested by the following Kuhn–Tucker condition on water releases:

$$\frac{\partial q_t^h}{\partial r_t} = \frac{\dfrac{\partial c_t^h}{\partial r_t} + \gamma_{t+1} + \psi - \delta_t^d + \delta_{t+1}^d}{\dfrac{\partial c_t^l(\cdot)}{\partial q_t^l} + \phi_t'} \tag{6.17}$$

In this instance, the current period shadow price on the ramp-down constraint, δ_t^d, increases water releases in the current period. However, higher water releases in the current period also make meeting the ramp-down requirement in the next period more difficult. With a binding next-period ramp-down requirement, as evidenced by its shadow price, δ_{t+1}^d, being greater than zero, water releases can be reduced in the current period to offset the effects of a binding ramp-down constraint in the current period. Such a situation could lead to lower thermal power generation in the current period followed by higher thermal power generation in the next period.

6.4   SUMMARY AND CONCLUSIONS

In this chapter we have incorporated environmental restrictions into the basic model of hydroelectric power provision presented in Chapter 5. These environmental constraints include total water release requirements, minimum and maximum hourly release constraints and ramp-up and ramp-down constraints. Some dams are subject to additional constraints including constraints on changes in reservoir elevation, but we have not considered that type of constraint here. We also included the possibility that the hydroelectric facility operator can meet demand with thermally generated electricity, an option that is quite common. Instead of using thermally generated power, some dam operators can supplement their power sales with power purchased for resale. The next chapter will present a model where the operator combines hydroelectric power generation with purchases for resale to meet demand.

7. Hydroelectric power provision by a United States Power Marketing Administration

Co-authored with Silvio J. Flaim and Richard E. Howitt[1]

The previous three chapters have presented a series of models of hydroelectric power provision. We now turn to a case study of a Power Marketing Administration (PMA) that operates hydroelectric power generating facilities and purchases power for resale to meet contractual commitments to long-term customers (usually electric utilities). A dynamic model of hydroelectricity generation is used to derive hourly hydroelectric power generation and purchases of replacement power to meet contractual demand in the presence of the sort of operational restrictions discussed in Chapters 5 and 6. In this chapter, we show how the hourly pattern of hydropower generation and purchases for resale depends on differences between on-peak and off-peak spot electricity prices coupled with the operating restrictions under which PMAs usually operate. The final part of this chapter will include a simulation of the Glen Canyon dam in Arizona.

7.1 POWER MARKETING ADMINISTRATIONS IN THE UNITED STATES

In the United States, PMAs such as the Western Area Power Administration schedule and dispatch releases from many hydroelectricity generating facilities that may be owned and operated by others. The actual amount of capacity and energy realized from these facilities within any period is determined in part by stochastic factors, such as weather, but the release pattern can be further constrained by the same types of operational restrictions discussed in previous chapters, namely, reservoir elevations, minimum flow requirements and ramping restrictions. The United States Fish and Wildlife Service (United States Department of the Interior) and other agencies establish these operational restrictions to mitigate the environmental effects associated with hydroelectric power generation.

PMAs often contract to provide more capacity and energy to their customers than can be generated from their facilities under average hydrological conditions. To make up this difference, PMAs must purchase and resell power from other sources. Although the cost of generating hydroelectric power does not depend on the time of day, the cost of purchasing power on the spot market can vary substantially between on-peak and off-peak periods. The PMA takes advantage of these temporal differences in price by purchasing power for resale during off-peak periods and concentrating hydroelectricity generation during on-peak periods to meet demand. This practice, which we term hydro-shifting (introduced in Edwards et al., 1992) minimizes costs to the PMA customer and allows the PMA customer to receive power during on-peak periods at below-market prices.

Investor-owned and publicly-owned utilities have for many years designed and operated hydropower facilities to respond to customers' on-peak load demands, and often use hydroelectric power and thermal generating capacity jointly to meet deliveries of power and energy specified in long-term contracts. Hence, the problem addressed in this chapter is an example of what is known as the hydro-thermal integration problem in the power engineering literature. Hydro-thermal integration can take different forms, such as pumped storage, and has been treated extensively in the engineering literature, including Jackson (1973) and Wood and Wollenberg (1996). Wood and Wollenberg discuss pumped storage and coordinating the activities of multiple hydroelectric plants that are downstream from one another, that is, hydraulically–coupled dams, a topic that we will take up in the next chapter. More general engineering analyses of hydroelectricity generation are extensive, and include Reznicek and Simonovic (1990), Saad et al. (1996) and Georgakakos et al. (1997a and 1997b). However, the analysis presented in this chapter differs from virtually all engineering-based analyses by considering how optimal dam operations are affected by downstream environmental management considerations.

To examine the pattern of water releases under typical market conditions, this chapter develops a dynamic model of hydroelectricity generation and purchases of replacement power that incorporates the pricing rules and operational restrictions imposed on these facilities. The operational restrictions considered are minimum release rates, ramping restrictions and total water release requirements. This chapter analyses how these restrictions affect generation and purchases for resale and hence affect resulting downstream flows. The main conclusions of this chapter include the following. First, in the absence of environmental restrictions on operations, providing power at minimum cost provides a rationale for concentrating hydroelectric power generation in the on-peak periods. Second, restrictions on release rates encourage the hydro operator to rely on more expensive resale power during the on-peak period than would otherwise be the case without these restrictions, even though significant hydro-shifting still occurs with these operational restrictions in place. Third, the practice of hydro-shifting runs counter to the usual least-cost utility planning practice of using cheaper power for baseload purposes and more expensive power to satisfy on-peak period demand. Fourth, ramping constraints, which may be initially thought to affect only on-peak period releases, can increase off-peak period releases, even when they are binding in the off-peak period only. Fifth, to the extent that the hydroelectric power operator is subject to a total water release requirement, for example, one that requires that so many acre-feet of water be released in a given period, the time horizon of the problem becomes finite which causes the shadow value of water (which here reflects the value of stored water in future-period hydroelectricity generation) to decline over the operating period, converging to zero in the final period. This stands in contrast to the usual result from the exhaustible resources literature that as a resource is used up, its shadow value increases.

Another motivation for this chapter is that managing water resources requires a balancing of many conflicting interests. A recent paper by Fisher et al. (1991) addressed fishery and water resource management in California and suggests gains from integrated management approaches. Germane to this chapter, management of hydroelectric power facilities might be better served by similar integrated approaches that balance the electricity requirements of end-users with environmental benefits and costs. A recent paper by

Edwards et al. (1996) estimated the effects of energy prices on fuel, water and crop substitution in irrigated agriculture.

In the next section we present the structure of the model, which is similar to that presented in the previous three chapters, but includes important differences which we shall point out. We shall then present and analyse the results of the optimization problem and then later present the results of simulations of a representative facility under alternative operational restrictions on the hydroelectric facility.

7.2   ASSUMPTIONS AND MODEL STRUCTURE

Following the models presented in previous chapters, the model is dynamic and runs for T days. In contrast to the models presented in previous chapters, we divide each of the t periods into two sub-periods, off-peak and on-peak periods. We can think of each of the T periods as days, and each day has two sub-periods, an off–peak period and an on-peak period. This division is somewhat arbitrary, but is analytically convenient and allows us to focus on how time-of-day price differences can influence dispatcher behaviour. Later on in the chapter when we present the simulation results, we will actually use a model that divides each day into 24 periods (hours), 12 of which are off-peak and the remaining 12 hours on-peak. We argue that for the theoretical model presented in this chapter, the essence of hydro dispatcher behaviour, including purchasing power for resale and storing water during the off-peak period for on-peak period releases, is captured in the current model which divides each day into one off–peak and one on–peak period. In the simulations presented later in this chapter, we divide each day into 24 hours, the first 12 of which are the off-peak period and the remaining 12 the on-peak period. In another departure from the models presented in previous chapters, we shall assume that spot electricity prices are exogenously determined, that is, the market share of the individual PMA is too small for their generation (or purchases for resale) to have any influence on spot prices. Moreover, we shall assume that the market price for electricity is lower during the off–peak period than during the on-peak period.

7.3 HYDROELECTRIC GENERATION AND RESALE POWER PROVISION

PMAs typically have three options with which to meet contractual demand: (1) they can purchase power on the spot market for resale to one or more of their customers; (2) they can release water and generate hydroelectric power; and (3) some combination of the two. For most facilities, the dispatcher faces water release requirements that include total monthly water releases, minimum hourly water release rates and hourly ramping restrictions set by other authorities.

This chapter divides the PMA's power supply into two components. The first is power purchased by the PMA on the spot market for resale to its customers. The second is power generated by releasing water. The quantity of power supplied by the PMA in any given day will be the sum of power sold in the off-peak and on-peak periods, given by equation (7.1):

$$Q_t = Q_t^b + Q_t^p \qquad (7.1)$$

where Q_t^b is the amount of off-peak period power provided and Q_t^p is the amount of on-peak period power provided in day t. The quantity that the PMA sells in the off-peak period of any day is the sum of power purchased for resale and the amount of hydroelectric power generated by releasing water in the off-peak period, which is given by equation (7.2):

$$Q_t^b = q_t^{rb} + q_t^{hb}(r_t^b, W_t) \qquad (7.2)$$

where q_t^{rb} is the amount of power purchased for resale in the off-peak period of day t, q_t^{hb} is the amount of hydro power generated and sold in the off-peak period of day t and r_t^b is the amount of water released for hydro power generation during the off-peak period. We denote the amount of water in the reservoir by W_t. We can interpret this amount as the live capacity of the reservoir. The effects that changes in reservoir content have on the productivity of water releases will be reflective of the head effects we have discussed in previous chapters. On-peak period power sold by the PMA is given by equation (7.3):

$$Q_t^P = q_t^{rp} + q_t^{hp} (r_t^P, W_t)$$ \hspace{2cm} (7.3)

where the variables are defined for the on-peak period in a manner analogous to their off-peak period counterparts. We assume that hydroelectricity generation is increasing in both arguments in both periods. However, the dynamic nature of the model presented in this chapter allows cumulative water releases, which are not fully offset by inflows of water to the reservoir, to reduce the water in the reservoir and the head of the dam. When this occurs, additional water releases will result in smaller increases in hydroelectric power generation than would occur at higher reservoir levels. For larger facilities, this effect will be negligible. For example, continuous releases from Glen Canyon dam in the spring of 1986 at 44 000 CFS (well above the maximum nameplate generator capacity of 33 000 CFS) reduced the head of the dam by about 6 inches during each 24-hour period. For smaller dams, this effect might be large enough to influence the pattern of water releases over the course of the month. We have discussed this issue in previous chapters, and Wood and Wollenberg discuss how the amount of generation possible from a cubic foot of water depends on the distance the water travels through the dam (via the penstock) and how this depends on the gross head of the dam. For example, Wood and Wollenberg state that

> [a] flow of 1 ft³/sec falling 1000 ft has the power equivalent of approximately 8.5 kW. If the flow-caused loss in head was 5%, or 5 ft, then the power equivalent for a flow of 1 ft³ of water per second with a net drop of 100-5, or 95 ft, would have the power equivalent of slightly more than 8 kW (8.5 X 95%) (1996, p. 212).

Nevertheless, the equation of motion for water is given by the following:

$$W_{t+1} = W_t - r_t^b - r_t^p + I_t \qquad (7.4)$$

where I_t is the amount of water that flows into the reservoir during period t. While there is a strong temptation to treat reservoir inflows as uncertain, we defer explicit treatment of uncertainty with respect to inflows, hydrology, prices, demand and other factors to possible future research. In addition, as we will discuss in the next two chapters, many of the Colorado River Storage Project dams, for example, are downstream from one another, including the Aspinall Unit near Gunnison, Colorado, which consists of the Blue Mesa, Morrow Point and Crystal dams. These dams are situated heel-to-toe in the upper reaches of the Black Canyon. For these facilities, side-stream inflows are so small that releases from the upper dam are virtually equivalent to inflows to the lower reservoir, leaving very little uncertainty about inflows to the reservoir. In addition, expectations about hydrology will be incorporated into the annual operating plans that come from the Bureau of Reclamation, which include monthly water release requirements that are accepted by those PMAs subject to these requirements. Many elements of uncertainty (particularly weather and hydrology) inherent in hydropower operations have been addressed in a number of papers, including Thomas et al. (1972) and Lane (1973).

Finally, the dispatcher is required to meet contractual obligations for power, so sales of hydroelectric power plus purchases for resale must be sufficient to satisfy contract demand requirements in each period. This requirement for the off-peak and on-peak periods of each day is given in equations (7.5) and (7.6):

$$\hat{Q}_t^b \leq q_t^{rb} + q_t^{hb}(r_t^b, H_t(W_t)) \qquad (7.5)$$

$$\hat{Q}_t^p \leq q_t^{rp} + q_t^{hp}(r_t^p, H_t(W_t)) \qquad (7.6)$$

where $\hat{Q}_t^b$ and $\hat{Q}_t^p$ are, respectively, the period t off-peak and on-peak period contractual demand. In some cases, PMAs have been able to purchase and resell spot power on the open market, with revenues from these sales used to offset the costs of operations. However, our analysis does not incorporate these sales, which historically account for about 6 per cent of their total operating revenues

7.4   PRODUCTION, GENERATION AND TRANSMISSION COSTS

From a statutory perspective, the PMAs are required to maximize the value of the facilities and services offered to their customers. Characterizing each of these functions and attempting to maximize the value of the facilities and include all market and non-market criteria would be intractable and is therefore beyond the scope of this chapter. Instead, we use a cost-minimization approach as a meaningful first step to limit the range of issues being examined and to focus on the trade-off between the economic and environmental attributes of the PMA operations. We assume that the PMA meets its total contractual commitment without deference to who qualifies to purchase PMA electricity and how the electricity could be priced under alternative scenarios of ownership and management. In addition, we do not attempt to include any sort of explicit environmental damage or benefit function. The environmental impacts of hydropower operations are not easily identified or measured, and can vary between facilities. In most cases, however, minimum flows are necessary to maintain downstream habitats, but some impacts are mutually exclusive, for example, many native fisheries typically require warm water, low water velocities and heavy sediment loads while many sport fisheries require clean, cold and fast-moving streams. In some cases, fluctuating flows can benefit some downstream areas by providing better habitat for terrestrial species and more food for their predators. In short, explicit treatment of environmental damages from dam operations is perhaps best treated on a qualitative and facility-specific basis. For similar reasons, we do not attempt to incorporate benefits coming from displaced emissions of carbon dioxide and sulphur dioxide. Finally, we do not examine issues relating to the sustained high rates of release at Glen Canyon during the spring of 1996, except to note that the purpose of such large sustained releases was to pass silt downstream to aid in beach formation and provide additional nutrients to aquatic species. See Collier et al. (1997) for a discussion of some of the effects of this flooding.

The economic literature on peak-load pricing, management, fuel-switching, alternative fuel sources and related issues is so extensive that we can only hope to list a few, including works by Steiner (1957), Panzar and Sibley (1978), Crew and Kleindorfer (1978), Hamlen and Tschirhart (1980), Brown and Sibley (1986) and Phillips (1988). We also recognize the growing literature on real-time pricing and other pricing innovations being brought to the fore in the face of the current trend towards deregulation of wholesale bulk power and retail markets. For example, the reader is referred to a recent article by Hanser et al. (1997) that addresses real-time pricing. However, the price of electricity generated at federally owned hydropower facilities is limited to the recovery of actual costs and is not adjusted to reflect market conditions. In addition, on-peak and off-peak spot prices are exogenous to any actions taken by the operators of these facilities. Moreover, hydropower produced at federally owned facilities (US Bureau of Reclamation hydroelectric power plants account for 23 per cent of the hydroelectric generating capacity) is exempt from the regulations and price- setting mechanisms of individual state public utility commissions (US Department of the Interior, Bureau of Reclamation, 1998).

With these caveats, we assume that the PMA is a price-taker during each period, that is, prices are exogenous and are not affected by the PMA's output, that the price that the PMA charges for its power is an average per kilowatt hour (kWh) charge, limited to cost recovery, and that the objective of the PMA is to meet its contractual commitments at minimum cost to its customers. Hydroelectric power is sold by the PMA to utilities at a price of p_t^h per kWh, regardless of time of day (we retain the time subscript for notational consistency, but assume that the hydroelectric power price will remain constant throughout the day). For resales, the PMA pays spot prices of p_t^{sb} during the off-peak period and p_t^{sp} during the on-peak period, resells this power to their customers at the spot price, but incurs an administrative resale cost of c_t^r per kWh for each resale and passes this resale cost through to their customers. We assume further that the cost of administering the resale does not differ between off-peak and on-peak periods. Since the PMA customer obtains hydroelectric power from the PMA at the PMA's cost, on-peak hydroelectric power purchased from the PMA during the on-peak period will be more valuable to the customer than if this power were either generated or purchased on the spot market by the customer directly. Recent wholesale rates for power sold at Palo Verde are \$38.16 per mWh (3.816 cents per kWh) for on-peak and \$14.19 per mWh (1.419 cents per kWh) for off-peak. This magnitude of difference is consistent with what we assume in our simulations presented later on (*Wall Street Journal*, 1996). In addition, a recent US General Accounting Office report cites average revenue per kWh for Western ranging from 1.13 to 2.6 cents, an average Western wholesale rate of 1.82 cents per kWh and an average wholesale rate for investor-owned utilities of 3.49 cents per kWh (US General Accounting Office, 1996).

7.5   OPTIMIZATION

The cost of providing power, which consists of the cost of generating hydroelectric power and purchasing power for resale in off-peak and on-peak periods, is given by equation (7.7):

$$
\begin{aligned}
C = \sum_{t=1}^{T} \{ p_t^h \cdot [q_t^{hb}(r_t^b, W_t) + q_t^{hp}(r_t^p, W_t)] \\
+ (p_t^{sb} + c_t^r) q_t^{rb} + (p_t^{sp} + c_t^r) q_t^{rp} \}
\end{aligned}
\tag{7.7}
$$

We minimize equation (7.7) subject to five sets of constraints. The first is the equation of motion, equation (7.4), which governs the relationship between reservoir level, water releases and inflows to the reservoir. The second is that the sum of hydroelectric power generation and purchases for resale are sufficient to satisfy customer demand in each period, given in equations (7.5) and (7.6). The third constraint is that the hydroelectricity dispatcher is limited in terms of the rate that water releases can either be increased or decreased in any period, which is embodied in equations (7.8) and (7.9):

$$
r_t^p - r_t^b \le r^u
\tag{7.8}
$$

$$
r_{t-1}^p - r_t^b \le r^d
\tag{7.9}
$$

Equation (7.8) limits the rate at which the dispatcher can ramp-up, that is, the rate at which water releases can be increased between periods, with the constraint given by r^u. Likewise, equation (7.9) limits the rate at which the dispatcher can ramp-down, that is, the rate at which water releases can be decreased between periods, which is limited to r^d. Presumably, on-peak water releases during a given day will exceed off-peak releases during the same day. Similarly, on-peak releases during one day (t) will exceed off-peak period releases for the following day ($t+1$). The ramping constraints may not be binding when these conditions do not hold. These constraints are imposed on the dispatcher to reduce short-term fluctuations in water releases which could cause downstream environmental damages. The fourth constraint requires the dispatcher to release a given minimum amount of water in each period, expressed as equations (7.10) and (7.11):

$$r_t^b \geq r^m \qquad\qquad (7.10)$$

$$r_t^p \geq r^m \qquad\qquad (7.11)$$

These constraints are imposed to maintain minimum flows necessary for downstream habitats. We assume that this minimum release constraint does not vary by period or by day and is given by r^m.

Although identifying the optimum release pattern over a period of several months is possible theoretically, PMAs are typically required to release specific amounts of water from each dam during each month of the year. These amounts are specified in the annual operating plans for the facilities and are established through negotiations with affected parties and multiple government agencies, and in some cases constrained by international law. Therefore, the final constraint is that a fixed quantity of water must be released during the month, given by the following:

$$\sum_{t=1}^{T} (r_t^b + r_t^p) = \tilde{R} \qquad\qquad (7.12)$$

where $\tilde{R}$ is the total amount of water to be released in the month.

7.6   OPTIMIZATION RESULTS

The operator chooses rates of water release and amount of power to purchase for resale in each period that minimize costs, given by equation (7.7), subject to equations (7.4) through (7.6) and equations (7.8) through (7.12).   The Lagrangian function is presented in equation (7.13):

$$
\begin{aligned}
J = \sum_{t=1}^{T-1} \{ & p_t^h \cdot [q_t^{hb}(r_t^b, W_t) + q_t^{hp}(r_t^p, W_t)] + (p_t^{rb} + c_t^r)q_t^{rb} + (p_t^{rp} + c_t^r)q_t^{rp} \\
& + \gamma_{t+1}(W_{t+1} - W_t + r_t^b + r_t^p - I_t) \\
& + \lambda_t^b(\hat{Q}_t^b - q_t^{hb}(r_t^b, W_t) - q_t^{rb}) \\
& + \lambda_t^p(\hat{Q}_t^p - q_t^{hp}(r_t^p, W_t) - q_t^{rp}) \\
& - \delta_t^u(r^u - (r_t^p - r_t^b)) \\
& - \delta_t^d(r^d - (r_{t-1}^p - r_t^b)) \\
& + \delta_t^{mb}(r^m - r_t^b) \\
& + \delta_t^{mp}(r^m - r_t^p) \} \\
& + p_T^h \cdot [q_T^{hb}(r_T^b, W_T) + q_T^{hp}(r_T^p, W_T)] \\
& + (p_T^{rb} + c_T^r)q_T^{rb} + (p_T^{rp} + c_T^r)q_T^{rp} \\
& + \lambda_T^b(\hat{Q}_T^b - q_T^{hb}(r_T^b, W_T) - q_T^{rb}) \\
& + \lambda_T^p(\hat{Q}_T^p - q_T^{hp}(r_T^p, W_T) - q_T^{rp}) \\
& - \delta_T^u(r^u - (r_T^p - r_T^b)) - \delta_T^d(r^d - r_T^p) \\
& + \delta_T^{mb}(r^m - r_T^b) + \delta_T^{mp}(r^m - r_T^p) \\
& - \theta_T(W_T - r_T^b - r_T^p + I_T) \\
& - \psi(\tilde{R} - \sum_{t=1}^{T}(r_t^b + r_t^p))
\end{aligned} \tag{7.13}
$$

In equation (7.13), we define γ_{t+1} as the discrete-time costate associated with the equation of motion and the λ_t's are the shadow prices on the demand constraints. We represent the shadow prices of the minimum flow requirements, ramp-up constraints and ramp-down constraints in equation (7.13), by the δ's. Finally, we introduce θ_T as the final period costate for the equation of motion and ψ as the costate for the total water release requirement constraint. The short time horizon of this problem, one month, leads us to ignore the effects of discounting. However, we recognize that a more general approach would consider the possibility that releases made earlier in the month be weighed more than releases made later on. We do not believe that introducing discounting would alter the basic conclusions of this chapter or dramatically affect the simulation results presented later on.

The discussion of the first-order conditions that follow and the simulations results reported in Section 7.9 will address two general issues. The first is how off-peak and on-peak price differences, coupled with the environmental constraints, affect the timing of water releases over the course of the day, that is, between the off-peak and on-peak hours, and the costs of changing the environmental constraints. More stringent environmental constraints, which will take the form of restrictions on release rates, can yield benefits in terms of reduced environmental damage or enhanced recreational activities, but might require that the PMA meet its demand requirement during the on-peak period with a greater proportion of more expensive on-peak resale power, rather than less expensive hydroelectric power. Thus the dispatcher faces a trade-off between environmental or recreational quality and low energy costs when deciding how to meet demand in each period.

The second issue involves the pattern of water releases over the course of the month and requires that we distinguish between stock and flow components of the value of water, a topic discussed previously in Chapter 4. The flow value of water is its value as an input in generating hydroelectric power. In contrast, the stock value is the value that the water has while in the reservoir on the generating efficiency of water releases. Naturally, the stock value of water will affect the flow value of water through effects that reservoir elevations have on dam head. Moreover, we shall see later that the stock value of water depreciates over the course of the month, and that this depreciation will ultimately have an effect on water releases throughout the course of the month.

The next section will develop the model under the assumption that none of the environmental constraints are binding. This allows us to examine the most basic issues involved in deciding how demand will be satisfied with the combination of hydroelectric power and purchases for resale power. In the following two sections, we focus on how water releases and purchases for resale are divided between off-peak and on-peak periods in the presence of binding environmental constraints. We will then address the issue of how water releases change over the course of the month by focusing on the behaviour of the shadow value of the water resource and how this value changes over the course of the month.

7.7   OPTIMAL HYDROELECTRIC POWER ALLOCATION WITHOUT ENVIRONMENTAL CONSTRAINTS

The first issue of the timing of the water releases can be addressed by applying the Kuhn–Tucker conditions and discrete–time maximum principle to (7.13) with respect to water releases and purchases for resale. If we assume that the environmental constraints are not binding, the Kuhn–Tucker conditions on off-peak period water releases are:

$$\frac{\partial J}{\partial r_t^b} = p_t^h \frac{\partial q_t^{hb}(\cdot)}{\partial r_t^b} + \gamma_{t+1} + \psi - \lambda_t^b \frac{\partial q_t^{hb}(\cdot)}{\partial r_t^b} \geq 0 \qquad (7.14)$$

$$r_t^b \frac{\partial J}{\partial r_t^b} = r_t^b [\cdot] = 0 \qquad (7.15)$$

In either period, water will be released to generate hydroelectric power as long as the marginal costs of releasing water, including the effects of the water and total release constraints, are no greater than the opportunity cost of meeting the demand requirement. According to equation (7.14), the marginal cost of hydropower generation in the off-peak period is the sum of the variable cost of hydroelectric power generation and distribution, $p_t^h \{\partial q_t^{hb}(\cdot)/\partial r_t^b\}$, the marginal cost of reduced future power generation due to lower water levels, γ_{t+1}, and the marginal cost of the total water release constraint, given by ψ. The term $\lambda_t^h \{\partial q_t^{hb}(\cdot)/\partial r_t^b\}$ is the opportunity cost of meeting the demand requirement in the off–peak period. We know from these conditions that if the demand constraint is not binding in the off–peak period, then the marginal cost of releasing water will be strictly greater than the opportunity cost of satisfying the demand requirement and no water will be released. The analogous set of Kuhn–Tucker conditions and results apply to on-peak period releases which are given in equations (7.16) and (7.17):

$$\frac{\partial J}{\partial r_t^p} = p_t^h \frac{\partial q_t^{hp}(\cdot)}{\partial r_t^p} + \gamma_{t+1} + \psi - \lambda_t^p \frac{\partial q_t^{hp}(\cdot)}{\partial r_t^p} \geq 0 \qquad (7.16)$$

$$r_t^p \frac{\partial J}{\partial r_t^p} = r_t^p[\cdot] = 0 \qquad (7.17)$$

Since the marginal value of the stock of water is the same in off-peak and on-peak periods and assuming an interior solution for water releases in both periods, we can combine equations (7.14) and (7.16) to obtain $(p_t^h - \lambda_t^b) \partial q_t^{hb}(\cdot)/\partial r_t^b = (p_t^h - \lambda_t^p) \partial q_t^{hp}(\cdot)/\partial r_t^p$. Since, for a given reservoir elevation, $\partial q_t^{hb}(\cdot)/\partial r_t^b = \partial q_t^{hp}(\cdot)/\partial r_t^p$, and given our assumption that the cost of generating hydroelectric power is invariant between the off-peak and on-peak periods, we obtain $\lambda_t^b = \lambda_t^p$, which tells us that without binding ramping and minimum release constraints, the opportunity cost of meeting the demand requirement is the same in both periods.

We can draw some additional inferences about the pattern of water releases and purchases for resale by considering the first-order conditions on purchases for resale in both on-peak and off-peak periods. Equations (7.18) and (7.19) show the first-order conditions for purchased spot power in the off-peak period:

$$\frac{\partial J}{\partial q_t^{rb}} = p_t^{sb} + c_t^r - \lambda_t^b \geq 0 \qquad (7.18)$$

$$q_t^{rb} \frac{\partial J}{\partial q_t^{rb}} = q_t^{rb}[\cdot] = 0 \qquad (7.19)$$

Equation (7.18) states that the cost of purchasing and reselling spot power can be greater or equal to the shadow value of satisfying the demand constraint. If power is purchased on the spot market during the off-peak period, equation (7.18) will hold with equality indicating that the shadow value is equal to the spot price plus resale cost. For the on-peak period, the corresponding first-order conditions on purchases for resale are given by:

$$\frac{\partial J}{\partial q_t^{rp}} = p_t^{rp} + c_t^r - \lambda_t^p \geq 0 \qquad (7.20)$$

$$q_t^{rp} \frac{\partial J}{\partial q_t^{rp}} = q_t^{rp}[\cdot] = 0 \qquad (7.21)$$

which can be given an analogous interpretation to equations (7.18) and (7.19). If the ramping and minimum release constraints are not binding and power is purchased in the off-peak period, then no power will be purchased for resale in the on-peak period. With power purchased in the off-peak period, we know from equation (7.18) that $p_t^{rb} + c_t^r = \lambda_t^b$. We can substitute our result that $\lambda_t^b = \lambda_t^p$ into equation (7.18) to obtain $p_t^{rb} + c_t^r = \lambda_t^p$. Since spot power is typically priced higher during the on-peak period, we also know that $p_t^{rp} > p_t^{rb}$, so it must be the case that $p_t^{rp} + c_t^r > \lambda_t^p$, which by equations (7.20) and (7.21) means that $q_t^{rp} = 0$. By similar logic, we can also state that if no power is purchased in the off-peak period, then no power will be purchased in the on-peak period either. This result is essentially a different way of stating the hydro-shifting argument, namely, that the difference between on-peak and off-peak spot prices leads the hydro dispatcher to satisfy off-peak demand with resale power (and possibly some hydroelectric power), and satisfy on-peak period demand with hydroelectric power only.

We can also use equations (7.14) to (7.21) to define a pure hydro-shifting case, that is, where no water is released in the off-peak period and no purchases for resale occur in the on-peak period. When $p_t^h(\partial q_t^{hb}(\cdot)/\partial r_t^b) + \gamma_{t+1} + \psi > \lambda_t^b(\partial q_t^{hb}(\cdot)/\partial r_t^b)$, we know from equation

(7.15) that $r_t^b = 0$. If purchases for resale occur in the off-peak period, so that $q_t^{rb} > 0$, we know from equation (6.19) that $p_t^{sb} + c_t^r = \lambda_t^b$. If water is released in the on-peak period, so that $r_t^P > 0$, we know from equation (7.17) that $p_t^h (\partial q_t^{hp}(\cdot)/\partial r_t^P) + \gamma_{t+1} + \psi = \lambda_t^P (\partial q_t^{hp}(\cdot)/\partial r_t^P)$. Finally, when $p_t^{TP} + c_t^r > \lambda_t^P$, we know from equation (7.21) that $q_t^{TP} = 0$. We can combine these results into the following relationship between the costs of resale power and the opportunity costs of the demand constraint for both periods: $p_t^{TP} + c_t^r > \lambda_t^P > \lambda_t^b = p_t^{sb} + c_t^r$. In short, sufficiently high on-peak spot prices for power will induce the dispatcher to meet on-peak demand with hydroelectric power and sufficiently low off-peak spot prices for power will induce the dispatcher to meet off-peak demand with purchases of resale power.

7.8   OPTIMAL HYDROELECTRIC POWER ALLOCATION WITH ENVIRONMENTAL CONSTRAINTS

The effect of binding ramping and minimum release constraints is twofold. First, non-zero values on the minimum flow and ramping constraint multipliers in equations (7.14) and (7.16) decouple the λ shadow value of hydro water between on-peak and off-peak periods. Since the environmental multipliers can change between on-peak and off-peak periods, the λ's will also change. Second, the shadow values on binding environmental constraints will re-link off-peak and on-peak period water releases in a different manner.

7.8.1   THE EFFECT OF MINIMUM RELEASE CONSTRAINTS

In equation (7.13) the minimum flow constraint for the off-peak period in time t has an associated multiplier δ_t^{mb} which will be non-zero when the constraint is binding. Assuming an interior solution, equations (7.14) and (7.16) can be re-expressed with binding minimum flow constraints as:

$$p_t^h \frac{\partial q_t^{hb}(\cdot)}{\partial r_t^b} + \gamma_{t+1} + \psi - \delta_t^{mb} = \lambda_t^b \frac{\partial q_t^{hb}(\cdot)}{\partial r_t^b} \qquad (7.22)$$

$$p_t^h \frac{\partial q_t^{hp}(\cdot)}{\partial r_t^p} + \gamma_{t+1} + \psi - \delta_t^{mp} = \lambda_t^p \frac{\partial q_t^{hp}(\cdot)}{\partial r_t^p} \qquad (7.23)$$

In the previous section we showed that, in the absence of environmental constraints and binding water releases, water releases would be concentrated in the on-peak periods and would not be used in the off-peak periods when resale purchases could supply the power. The introduction of minimum flow constraints means that enough water must be released in the off-peak period to satisfy the constraint. The cost of being forced to use scarce water to generate hydroelectric power in the off-peak period is reflected in the multiplier δ_t^{mb}. The multiplier modifies the off-peak period opportunity cost for releases downward. Two changes are worth noting. First, the equality of the release opportunity cost for on-peak and off-peak periods that holds without environmental constraints, no longer holds. In particular, using the same assumption of equal marginal productivity of hydro power, equations (7.22) and (7.23) can be rearranged to show that:

$$\lambda_t^b \frac{\partial q_t^{hb}}{r_t^b} + \delta_t^{mb} = \lambda_t^p \frac{\partial q_t^{hp}}{r_t^p} + \delta_t^{mp} \qquad (7.24)$$

which reduces to

$$\lambda_t^b \frac{\partial q_t^{hb}}{r_t^b} + \delta_t^{mb} = \lambda_t^p \frac{\partial q_t^{hp}}{r_t^p} \qquad (7.25)$$

in the likely event that the minimum release requirement is binding in the off-peak period, but not in the on-peak period, as would be the case under pure hydro-shifting. Second, adding a binding minimum release requirement in the off-peak period modifies our previous result involving resale purchases in the off-peak period. Recall that when resale purchases occur in the off-peak period without a binding minimum release constraint, we know from equations (7.18) and (7.19) that the opportunity cost of off-peak period power is determined by resale power costs ($p_t^{tb} + c_t^r = \lambda_t^b$). However, a binding minimum release constraint reduces the opportunity cost of meeting the demand requirement and, depending on the shadow value of the minimum release constraint, can reduce off-peak purchases for resale to zero.

7.8.2 THE EFFECT OF CONSTRAINTS ON THE RATE OF CHANGE OF FLOW

Ramping constraints restrict the rate of change of flow and thus restrict surges in water or rapid changes in temperature. It is possible that ramping and minimum flow constraints can hold simultaneously, but for simplicity we will consider their effects separately. Since the ramping constraints involve both off-peak and on-peak release rates, they modify both the on-peak and off-peak opportunity costs of releases. Under binding ramping-up constraints and assuming an interior solution, equations (7.14) and (7.16) are rewritten as:

$$p_t^h \frac{\partial q_t^{hb}(\cdot)}{\partial r_t^b} + \gamma_{t+1} + \psi - \delta_t^u = \lambda_t^b \frac{\partial q_t^{hb}(\cdot)}{\partial r_t^b} \qquad (7.26)$$

$$p_t^h \frac{\partial q_t^{hp}(\cdot)}{\partial r_t^p} + \gamma_{t+1} + \psi + \delta_t^u = \lambda_t^p \frac{\partial q_t^{hp}(\cdot)}{\partial r_t^p} \qquad (7.27)$$

Using the same assumption of equal marginal productivity of hydropower, equations (7.25) and (7.26) can be combined to show that:

$$\lambda_t^b + \delta_t^u \frac{\partial r_t^b}{\partial q_t^{hp}} = \lambda_t^p - \delta_t^u \frac{\partial r_t^p}{\partial q_t^{hp}} \qquad (7.28)$$

which can be rearranged to form:

$$\lambda_t^p - \lambda_t^b = 2\delta_t^u \frac{\partial r_t^p}{\partial q_t^h} \tag{7.29}$$

The effect of the ramping-up constraint is to modify the opportunity cost of releases in both periods. Equation (7.27) shows that the cost of meeting the ramping constraint encourages the use of releases in the off-peak period by increasing the opportunity cost of power and reducing the release level in on-peak periods by lowering the opportunity cost of power. Equation (7.28) shows that the cost wedge caused by the ramping constraint is split evenly between the two adjacent periods. In the empirical example in the next section, the number of periods is expanded and the results show how the ramping constraints are accommodated by adjustment to both on-peak and off-peak releases.

This discussion of the optimal conditions has focused on the cost wedge that environmental constraints drive between the unconstrained switching of hydropower and resale power among on-peak and off-peak periods. The necessary conditions show that without environmental constraints, the opportunity cost of hydroelectric power is equal in on-peak and off-peak periods, and set by the higher sale price in on-peak periods. Given constrained hydro releases, the optimal allocation will switch to hydropower for on-peak periods and resale power for off-peak periods.

The introduction of a minimum flow constraint separates the on-peak and off-peak period opportunity cost and forces a lower opportunity cost of releases in the off-peak period, allowing a mix of resale and hydropower to be optimal in the off-peak period. The cost of this constraint is shown to be a function of the differential between on-peak and off-peak power prices and the level of the constraint. Ramping constraints also modify the release opportunity costs, but in this case both the on-peak and off-peak opportunity costs are changed and the cost of the constraint is optimally split between the off-peak and on-peak periods. The relative importance of the environmental constraints on the optimal allocation of water releases is demonstrated empirically in the following section.

7.8.3 DYNAMIC CONDITIONS GOVERNING THE WATER RESOURCE

In any given period, the stock value of the water will reflect its value in increasing the generating efficiency of future releases, via effects that storing water has on the head of the dam. Moreover, any contribution hydroelectric power makes towards meeting demand allows the PMA to avoid having to make spot market purchases. In deciding how much water to release in the current period, the hydro dispatcher must weigh the benefits of current generation against the costs of future purchases for resale and reduced hydroelectricity generating efficiency, made necessary by releasing water in the current period. Both considerations affect how water releases in any given day will be divided between off-peak and on-peak periods and how water releases will be distributed over the course of the month. During the day, the dispatcher has incentives to store water during the off-peak period for release during the on-peak period, but as the month proceeds, the benefits of storing water diminish as the number of future periods decrease.

For a given reservoir size, releasing water in the current period costs the PMA customer p_t^h times the amount of electricity generated, but contributes to meeting the demand constraint without having to purchase resale power on the spot market. From equations (7.20) and (7.21), the cost of purchases for resale in the on-peak period $(p_t^{\varpi} + c_t^r)$ sets the opportunity cost of meeting the demand requirement (λ_t^p). Since the on-peak period spot price of power will usually exceed the cost of hydroelectric power, additional reservoir water will benefit the PMA customer by $\lambda_t^p - p_t^h$ for a given rate of water release. Therefore, additional water in the reservoir provides additional generation that contributes to the demand requirement, allows the PMA customer to avoid spot market purchases, but costs p_t^h times the amount of electricity generated. Since demand and spot prices will typically be lower during off-peak periods, the advantages of stored water will likely be lower. Nevertheless, the dynamic conditions governing the change in the marginal cost of water are embodied in equation (7.30):

$$\frac{\partial J}{\partial W_t} = -(\lambda_t^p - p_t^h)\frac{\partial q_t^{hp}(\cdot)}{\partial H_t(\cdot)}\frac{\partial H_t(\cdot)}{\partial W_t}$$

$$-(\lambda_t^b - p_t^h)\frac{\partial q_t^{hb}(\cdot)}{\partial H_t(\cdot)}\frac{\partial H_t(\cdot)}{\partial W_t} - (\gamma_{t+1} - \gamma_t) = 0 \tag{7.30}$$

which we can give the following interpretation. The term $-(\lambda_t^p - p_t^h)\left(\partial q_t^{hp}(\cdot)/\partial H_t(\cdot)\right)\left(\partial H_t(\cdot)/\partial W_t\right)$ represents the marginal benefit that additional dam head has to the utility in the on-peak period for a given rate of water release. An analogous interpretation can be given to the term, $-(\lambda_t^b - p_t^h)\left(\partial q_t^{hb}(\cdot)/\partial H_t(\cdot)\right)\left(\partial H_t(\cdot)/\partial W_t\right)$, for the off-peak period. Taken together, these terms represent the value of having additional water in the reservoir in the current period. The last term in this equation, $-(\gamma_{t+1} - \gamma_t)$, represents the change in the shadow value of the water and reflects the net contribution of the water in future periods. Equation (7.29) can be rearranged as a difference equation (for $\Delta\gamma = \gamma_{t+1} - \gamma_t$) and solved to express the current-period shadow value of water in terms of the value that the stored water has on meeting remaining future period demand requirements, less the cost of the additional hydroelectric generation in these periods.

Over time, the benefits of storing water will decrease. In the last period, water has value only for its generating value in that period. We also see that γ_t is the sum of these benefits for the remaining periods, which decline as we approach the end of the month. In the absence of environmental constraints, the terminal costate is shown to be equal to minus the cost of purchasing and reselling power in the on-peak period in time T. This reduction over time in the marginal value of stored water leads to a gradual change in the first-order conditions determining the switch between purchasing spot power and generating hydroelectric power. Over time, the difference between the marginal cost of hydroelectric power and purchasing power decreases. This change in the first-order conditions between the two power sources can be interpreted as an adjustment to the reduced benefits of storing water.

$$\gamma_t = \sum_{t=1}^{T-1} [(\lambda_t^p - p_t^h) \frac{\partial q_t^{hp}(\cdot)}{\partial H_t(\cdot)} \frac{\partial H_t(\cdot)}{\partial W_t}$$

$$+ (\lambda_t^b - p_t^h) \frac{\partial q_t^{hb}(\cdot)}{\partial H_t(\cdot)} \frac{\partial H_t(\cdot)}{\partial W_t}]$$

$$+ (\lambda_T^p - p_T^h) \frac{\partial q_T^{hp}(\cdot)}{\partial H_T(\cdot)} \frac{\partial H_T(\cdot)}{\partial W_T}$$

$$+ (\lambda_T^b - p_T^h) \frac{\partial q_T^{hb}(\cdot)}{\partial H_T(\cdot)} \frac{\partial H_T(\cdot)}{\partial W_T}$$

(7.31)

7.9 SIMULATIONS

The simulations presented in this section are loosely based on the Glen Canyon dam located on the Colorado River in Arizona. Glen Canyon, one of the largest dams in the United States, consists of eight generators driven by eight 155 500 horsepower turbines. Total nameplate generating capacity is 1296000 kilowatts. It is one of the Colorado River Storage Project (CRSP) dams and its generators provide more storage capacity than the rest of the CRSP dams combined. The Glen Canyon power plant is operated under the Glen Canyon Dam Final Environmental Impact Statement and Record of Decision which places operating restrictions on minimum and maximum release rates and ramp-up and ramp-down restrictions.

In these simulations, we assume that the dispatcher faces a demand requirement that ranges from 334 megawatts during the off-peak period to 617 megawatts during the on-peak period. Contractual demand can be met with either power purchased for resale, hydroelectric power, or some combination of each. For these simulations, we assume that the wholesale spot price of electricity ranges from $30 per mega–watt hour (mWh) to $80 per mWh. Purchases for resale are executed at cost, but an administrative cost of $2 per mWh is imposed on these resales. Sales of hydropower can occur in both periods and we assume that the PMA charges $15 per mWh for hydroelectric power regardless of the time–of–day. The baseline simulation assumes that the only constraint is a total monthly water release requirement. The second simulation adds a minimum hourly release rate requirement. The third simulation adds a maximum release constraint. The fourth and fifth simulations add a ramp-up constraint and ramp-down constraint, respectively. All of the simulations reported in this chapter were conducted using the General Algebraic Modelling System (GAMS) software program (Brooke et al., 1998).

To perform the simulations, we assume that hydroelectric power is generated according to $q_t^h = r_t H_t / \alpha$, where α is the production function coefficient we discussed in Chapter 4, H_t is dam head and W_t is reservoir content. For these simulations, we assume a value of $\alpha = 13$. Head was estimated econometrically from data provided by the US Bureau of Reclamation. The equation used was of the form $H_t = \beta_0 + \beta_1 W_t$. The level of water in the reservoir is assumed to be governed by equation (7.4). For these simulations, inflows were allowed to vary from hour to hour and were assumed to be distributed normally with a mean of 12000 CFS and a standard deviation of 2000 CFS.

This model runs for one week (168 hours), running from Sunday to Saturday. Since the first and last days of the week in the simulation are weekend days, these days represent off-peak days and spot electricity prices are assumed to be lower on these days. On days two to six (Monday to Friday), we have a characteristic off-peak period (with low spot prices) and an on-peak period (with higher spot prices). Figure 7.1 shows how hourly spot prices behave over the seven-day period.

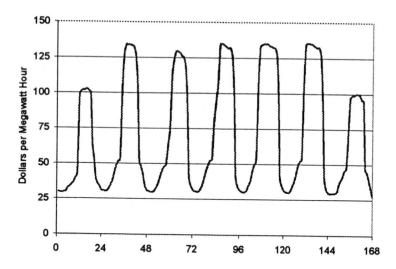

Figure 7.1 Hourly spot prices

Since these spot prices vary directly with demand (or load), demand will exhibit behaviour analogous to that of prices. Figure 7.2 shows demand over the same 168 hour period.

We assume that the hydroelectric power dispatcher chooses hourly rates of water release and purchases for resale to meet customer demand at minimum cost to its customers, usually electric utilities (Western also sells hydroelectric power to other organizations, including government military installations). Given the fact that the hydroelectric power is sold at Western's system-wide rate, which does not depend on time of day, the PMA will have an incentive to provide cheaper hydroelectric power to their customers at those times when the cheaper hydroelectric power provides the greatest benefit, namely during the on-peak hours when spot electricity prices are at their highest point. This allows Western's customers to receive hydroelectric power during those times when electricity purchased on the wholesale spot market would be substantially more expensive, thereby avoiding higher on-peak wholesale spot market electricity prices.

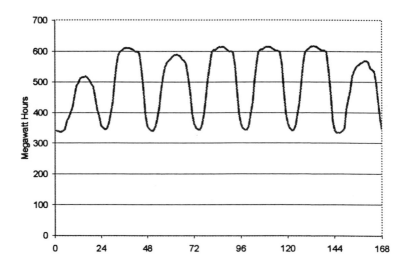

Figure 7.2 Hourly demand

7.9.1   BASELINE SIMULATION

The first (baseline) simulation assumes no restrictions other than the requirement that the operator release 100 000 acre-feet of water over the course of the week. According to this simulation and as illustrated in Figure 7.3, on-peak water release rates are as high as 14 00 CFS. At this rate of release, approximately 608 megawatt-hours of electricity are generated. During those hours when hydroelectric power is not generated, demand is met with purchases for resale. This simulation illustrates the notion of hydro-shifting, whereby the operator stores water during the off-peak periods for release (and generation) during on-peak periods and relies on purchases for resale to satisfy customer load during off-peak periods. Given that the objective of the hydroelectric operator is to meet the contract commitment at minimum cost to the Western customer, the operator meets this commitment at minimum cost by storing water in the reservoir during off-peak periods and releasing this water for hydroelectricity generation, and resulting sales, during on-peak periods. In the meantime, off-peak power is provided largely by purchases for resale at lower off-peak spot prices.

Figure 7.4 compares hourly hydroelectric power generation with the hourly pattern of purchase for resale to illustrate this notion.

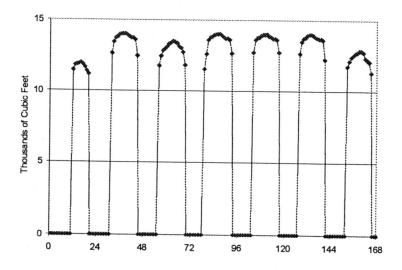

Figure 7.3 Hourly water release rates: baseline simulation

One of the important features of the models presented in this book is the relationship between the variables that govern the water resource. In particular, we have paid considerable attention to the effects that changes in release rates have on reservoir content and elevation and dam head and how the latter influences the productivity of water releases. Let us see how these variables behave in the baseline simulation. Given our assumption about inflows, namely that they occur at a mean of 12 000 CFS with a standard deviation of 2000 CFS, we should expect the content and head of the reservoir to rise over the course of the month (even though water releases can exceed twice that amount in the simulations, the total water release requirement limits such high rates to just a few hours each day). Moreover, inflows at an average rate of 12 000 CFS mean that inflows total 164 000 acre-feet over the course of the week, which exceeds the total water release requirement of 100 000 acre-feet that we have assumed in these simulations.

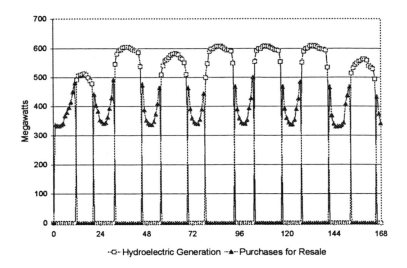

Figure 7.4 Generation and purchases for resale: baseline simulation

Figure 7.5 shows reservoir content and head over the course of the week. As would be suggested by the pattern of water releases and rates of inflow into the reservoir, content head rises during the simulation, but these increases are interrupted by brief drops that occur during the on-peak hours, as the water release rates are ramped up to meet demand.

This should also cause the generating efficiency of the dam to rise over the course of the month. For lack of a better measure, we define efficiency in simple input–output terms, namely as hydroelectric power generation divided by water release. Since the simulation has hours where no water is released, we can calculate generator efficiency only during those hours when water is released, namely during the on-peak hours. As a result, Figure 7.6 shows many gaps in the efficiency measure when release rates are zero. However, during the on-peak hours, we see that generating efficiency ranges from 42.9 to 43.8, a small range, but a range that suggests that the head effects that we have discussed exist and will have some bearing on the decision of when to release water. The reader should also notice that, in addition to the general rise in generating efficiency that occurs over the course of the week, small reductions in efficiency occur during the on-peak hours of each day. This is the result of high on-peak rates of water release (that reduce content and head) not being offset by high enough inflows to maintain dam head. This explains the slight ratcheting-down in efficiency that occurs during the on-peak hours that is shown in the figure.

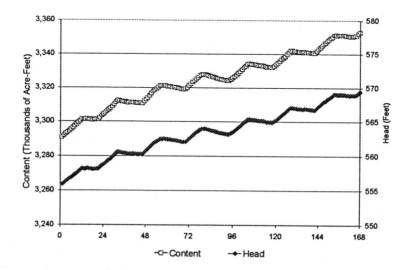

Figure 7.5 Reservoir content and dam head: baseline simulation

Finally, we consider the shadow price of the water resource. In this and previous chapters, we argued that, as the hours approach the end of the simulation period, the total water release requirement becomes exhausted. As a result, there is less to be gained by withholding water for future releases, particularly if the motive is to store the water to boost on-peak period generating efficiencies with which to maximize generation. This argument suggests that the shadow value of the water resource would fall to zero as the simulation draws to a close. This is illustrated in Figure 7.7 which shows how the shadow price changes over the week.

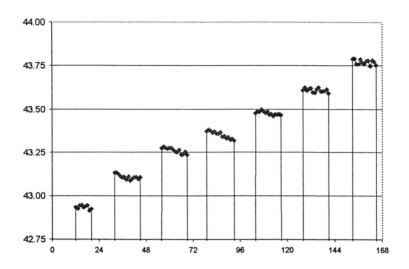

Figure 7.6 Generating efficiency: baseline simulation

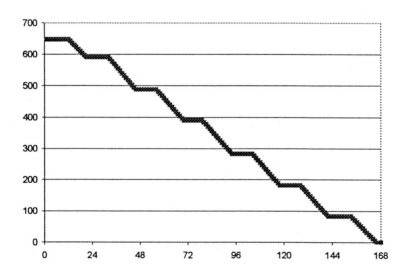

Figure 7.7 Shadow value of water: baseline simulation

7.9.2 REPRESENTATIVE DAY

We can create an additional figure that shows what happens during a representative day of the week. This figure is based on averaging the first hour of each day and letting the result represent behaviour for the first hour of the representative day, averaging the second hour of each day and letting the result of that calculation represent behaviour for the second hour of the representative day and so on to create an average day. Figure 7.8 shows how hourly release rates and purchases for resale vary over the course of the representative 20-hour period under the baseline simulation.

This figure illustrates the notion of hydro-shifting. During off-peak hours, water is stored in the reservoir and demand is met through purchases for resale. As we move into the on-peak hours of the representative day, water is released for hydroelectric power generation and demand is met with hydroelectric power. In the meantime, purchases for resale drop to zero during the on-peak hours.

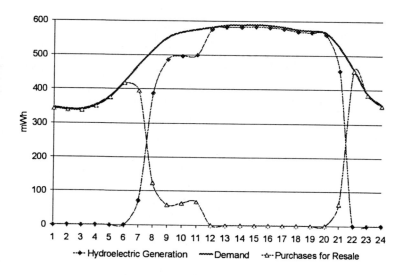

Figure 7.8 Hydroelectric generation, demand and purchases for resale: baseline simulation

7.9.3 MINIMUM RELEASE REQUIREMENT SIMULATION

In the second simulation, we impose a minimum release requirement that ranges from 5000 to 8000 CFS over the course of the week. Minimum release requirements are usually imposed to ensure that downstream environmental, wildlife and recreation objectives are satisfied (imagine fly–fishing without water). In any case, given that the operator still has to meet the total water release requirement, the new minimum release requirement is going to force the operator to redistribute water releases over the course of the week. However, the objective of the operator remains the same, that is, to meet hourly contract commitments at minimum cost to the customer. Once the minimum release requirement is met, the operator will release as much water as it can during on-peak times and does so as illustrated in Figure 7.9.

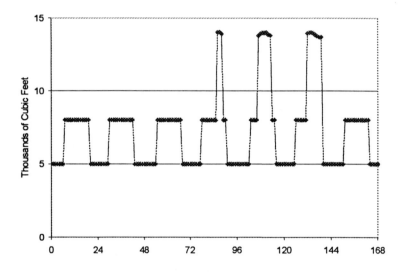

Figure 7.9 Water release rates: minimum release constraint

If we compare this figure to Figure 7.3 (which shows hourly water release rates under the baseline simulation), we see that the fluctuations in water release rates are far less pronounced. The first three days and the last day of the week see releases either at 5000 CFS or 8000 CFS. On Wednesday to Friday, water release rates are either at 5000 CFS, 8000 CFS, or they jump to a maximum rate of just over 14 000 CFS where they stay until demand drops off.

7.9.4   MAXIMUM RELEASE CONSTRAINT SIMULATION

In the next simulation, we add a maximum release constraint to the existing total water release and minimum water release constraints. In this simulation, the operator is not allowed to exceed 12 500 CFS during the week. As in the previous two simulations, the operator has to meet the total water release requirement. The minimum and maximum release constraints cause the peak water release rates in the previous simulation to fall to the new maximum. However, during the on-peak hours, the operator can sustain high water release rates over more hours of the on-peak period. The results of this simulation are presented in Figure 7.10.

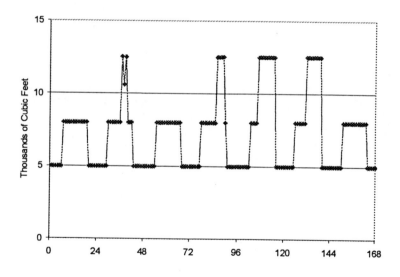

Figure 7.10 Water release rates: minimum and maximum release constraints

7.9.5   RAMP–UP CONSTRAINT SIMULATION

A close look at the above figure reveals that during those hours when the operator brings releases up to the maximum rate, the operator moves to that rate within one period. The next simulation adds a ramp–up constraint which limits the rate at which release rates can increase to 2500 CFS. The results of this simulation are illustrated in Figure 7.11. In this simulation, the operator brings on-peak release rates up to the maximum allowable over a period of about four hours. However, notice the following. Each day begins with the operator releasing water at a rate of 5000 CFS. But instead of immediately jumping to the minimum of 8000 CFS, there is an intermediate release rate (in this case, 5500 CFS) that allows the operator to get to the higher minimum hourly release rate of 8000 CFS without violating the ramp–up restriction of 2500 CFS. Without taking this intermediate step-up in water release rates, the operator would have to violate the minimum hourly release requirement in order to satisfy the ramp-up constraint.

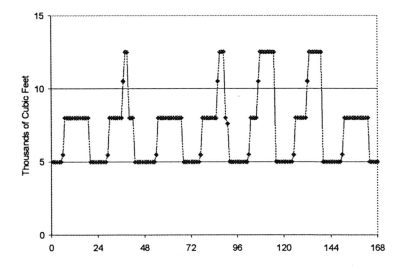

Figure 7.11 Water release rates: minimum and maximum release constraints and ramp-up constraint.

7.9.6 RAMP–DOWN CONSTRAINT SIMULATION

In our final simulation, we add the ramp-down constraint which limits the rate at which water release rates can be reduced. We set this constraint at 2500 CFS. As is shown in Figure 7.12, all of these constraints serve to dampen the rate at which water release rates change from hour to hour. Interestingly, this simulation is characterized by intermediate release rates as they ramp up (as in the previous simulation) and as the operator ramps down. On the second day, for example, the operator reaches the on-peak maximum release rate of 12 500 CFS, then reduces the release rate to 10 000 CFS for one hour, then drops to 5500 for one hour and then drops to the minimum of 5000 CFS. A similar ramping-down occurs on each of the fourth to sixth days of the week.

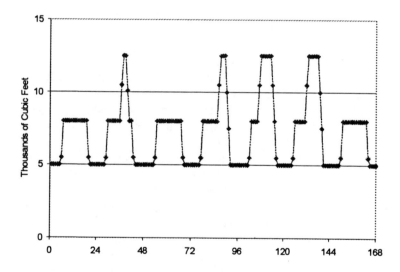

Figure 7.12 Demand, hydroelectric generation and resales: minimum and maximum release constraints and ramp–up and ramp–down constraints

7.10 ESTIMATING THE RECREATIONAL BENEFITS OF ENVIRONMENTAL CONSTRAINTS

The simulations presented in this chapter show how operating restrictions can reduce the rate of flow below a dam and reduce the fluctuations in downstream flow. Is there some way to estimate the benefits of these environmental restrictions? In this section we will present an example of how one might estimate the recreational benefits for one particular recreational activity, namely fishing. While there are many other recreational uses of rivers, including white-water rafting and many other environmental and ecological benefits of controlling downstream flows, we shall focus on just one of these potential benefits, knowing full well that there are many others that are not considered in this section.

One of the most common downstream recreational activities is fishing. The quality of downstream fishing, however, can vary greatly depending on downstream conditions. Very low downstream flows can reduce downstream fish populations so low as to make fishing unattractive. Very high downstream flows can make fishing, fly-fishing in particular, not only dangerous but can also render the probability of catching fish lower. Moreover, whether flows are constant or fluctuating, for a given rate of flow, can also affect the quality of the fishing experience.

Constraints that limit the rate of, and fluctuations in, water releases will affect the quality of recreational fishing activities and how individuals value these activities. Two studies, one by Bishop et al. (1987) and one by Carlson and Palmer (1997), addressed the issue of how rates of flow and fluctuations in flow affect valuations of recreational use values. In the first study, the authors estimated recreational use values for angling below Glen Canyon dam. The second study used the results of the first study and developed methods to transfer these results to estimating recreational use values below the Flaming Gorge dam. Since the simulations presented in this chapter focus on Glen Canyon, we will consider the recreational use values estimated in the first study.

Table 7.1 summarizes surplus values for angling below Glen Canyon dam. These estimates are taken from Carlson and Palmer (page 37), but are based on estimates originally made by Bishop et al. There are two factors that determine the recreational use value of downstream angling. The first is the average daily rate of flow. In Table 7.1, use values are estimated for average daily rates of flow ranging from 1000 to 30 000 CFS. The second factor is whether the flows are constant or fluctuating. A day characterized by fluctuating flows is defined as a day where the difference between the maximum and minimum rate of flow is greater than 10 000 CFS. For example a day with 0 CFS flows in the morning and 15 000 CFS in the afternoon would be classified as a day characterized by fluctuating flows. A day characterized by constant flows is defined as one where the difference between the maximum and minimum rate of flow is less than 10 000 CFS. If we take a closer look at the table, we notice recreational use values under fluctuating and constant flow regimes, with these values estimated by trip and by day for average daily flow rates ranging from 1000 to 30 000 CFS.

If we consider a day with an average daily flow of 10 000 CFS, the recreational use value of fishing will depend on whether the daily flows can be classified as fluctuating or constant. If flows vary by more than 10 000 CFS over the course of the day, but average 10 000 CFS, each fishing trip would have a value of $100 and each day of fishing would have a value of $41.20. If flows were classified as constant, then each fishing trip would have a value of $149 and each day of fishing would have a value of $59.60.

Notice that for a given average daily flow rate, the day with constant flows is more valuable than the day with fluctuating flows. However, these estimated recreational use values also capture the effect that very high average daily flow rates have on the value of angling. Notice that once we reach an average daily flow rate of 10 000 CFS, the per-trip and per-day values decline as the average daily flow rate increases and this is true regardless of whether flows are fluctuating or constant. For other kinds of recreational activities, higher average daily flow rates might actually increase the recreational use values. For example, the recreational use values for rafting are higher, the higher the average daily rate of flow.

Table 7.1 Summary of surplus values for angling below Glen Canyon dam (1991 dollars)

Flow (000 CFS)	Fluctuating Flows Per Trip	Fluctuating Flows Per Day	Constant Flows Per Trip	Constant Flows Per Day	Flow (000 CFS)	Fluctuating Flows Per Trip	Fluctuating Flows Per Day	Constant Flows Per Trip	Constant Flows Per Day
1	NA	-	61	24.4	16	94	37.6	134	53.6
2	NA	-	71	28.4	17	93	37.2	132	52.8
3	81	32.4	81	32.4	18	91	36.4	129	51.6
4	84	33.6	90	36.0	19	90	36.0	127	50.8
5	87	34.8	100	40.0	20	88	35.2	124	49.6
6	90	36.0	110	44.0	21	87	34.8	122	48.8
7	94	37.6	120	48.0	22	85	34.0	119	47.6
8	97	38.8	130	52.0	23	84	33.6	117	46.8
9	100	40.0	140	56.0	24	82	32.8	114	45.6
10	103	41.2	149	59.6	25	81	32.4	111	44.4
11	102	40.8	147	58.8	26	79	31.6	108	43.2
12	100	40.0	144	57.6	27	78	31.2	105	42.0
13	99	39.6	142	56.8	28	76	30.4	102	40.8
14	97	38.8	139	55.6	29	-	-	98	39.2
15	96	38.4	137	54.8	30	-	-	95	38.0

Source: Carlson and Palmer (1997).

Table 7.2 contains the number of angler trips below Glen Canyon dam, by month, in 1991. According to this table, the month of July saw 1308 angling trips below Glen Canyon dam. The baseline simulation reported above had an average representative daily flow of about 7274 CFS. The difference between the minimum and maximum representative daily flow was 13 461. As a result, the baseline would be considered a simulation characterized by fluctuating flows. If we apply these figures to the recreational use value estimates in Table 7.1, we find that each angling trip is worth about $94.82 (we linearly interpolate to obtain the intermediate value) and each day of fishing is worth about $37.93. If this simulation occurred during the month of July, then the recreational use value of angling flow Glen Canyon dam would be $94.82 X 1,308 or $124 025 over the course of July.

Table 7.2 Angler trips below Glen Canyon dam, 1991

Month	Trips	Month	Trips
January	624	July	1308
February	997	August	900
March	1237	September	1016
April	1285	October	1491
May	1639	November	870
June	1006	December	529

Source: Michael Welsh, personal correspondence.

Let us compare recreational use values under the baseline to the last simulation we conducted, namely that with minimum and maximum release rate constraints and ramp–up and ramp–down constraints. For this simulation, let us further compare two different days. The first day shows hourly water release rates vary from 5000 CFS to 8000 CFS and release rates average 6670 CFS. Given the low range of hourly release rates (the difference between the highest and lowest release rate being less than 10 000 CFS), this would be a day characterized by constant flows. With an average hourly release rate of 6670 CFS, we obtain a valuation of $116.70 per trip (as in the baseline, we linearly interpolate to obtain the intermediate value), or $46.68 per day. With 1308 trips, we obtain a total estimated recreational use value of $156 644 in July.

For another comparison, consider the fifth day of the week of this simulation. On this day, water release rates range from 5000 CFS to 12 500 CFS, so we can still categorize this day as a constant flow day, but the average hourly release rate for this day is 7880 CFS. Using the values from Table 7.1, we obtain a recreational use value of $128.80 (again, we linearly interpolate to obtain the intermediate value), or $51.52 per trip. With 1308 trips, we obtain a total estimated recreational use value of $177 744.

We summarize these results in Table 7.3. As is clear from the table, the recreational use values for angling increase as we move from the baseline simulation (with no operating restrictions save the total water release constraint) to the simulation with all of the operating restrictions. Moreover, we see that the recreational use value does not always increase as the degree of fluctuations in water release rates decrease. In comparing the first and the fifth day of the last simulation, we see that the slightly higher average hourly release rates actually make angling more attractive, not less attractive. If we had started out with a baseline that had an average hourly release rate in the higher ranges, for example, 25 000 CFS, then a binding maximum release constraint would most likely result in higher recreational use values. We also have to keep in mind that this example is for downstream angling only. White-water rafting, another popular recreational activity, improves in quality (and hence in recreational use value) as water release rates increase.

Table 7.3 Summary of recreational use value estimates

	Baseline	First Day Simulation	Fifth Day Simulation
Minimum Flow Rate	0 CFS	5 000 CFS	5 000 CFS
Maximum Flow Rate	13 461 CFS	8 000 CFS	12 500 CFS
Difference	13 461 CFS	3 000 CFS	7 500 CFS
Flow Regime	Fluctuating	Constant	Constant
Average Hourly Rate of Flow	7 274 CFS	6 670 CFS	7 880 CFS
Per Trip Value	$94.82	$116.70	$128.80
Per Day Value	$37.93	$46.68	$51.52
Aggregate Value (1308 trips)	$124 025	$156 644	$177 744

7.11   SUMMARY AND CONCLUSIONS

This chapter has presented a case study of a Power Marketing Administration that meets contractual commitments to customers by combining hydroelectric power with purchases for resale. We derived a series of theoretical conditions that determine when water will be released for generation and when demand will be met with purchases for resale. We found that, given the manner in which the power is priced to the customer, the PMA has an incentive to hydro-shift, that is, to store water during off-peak hours for release and generation during on-peak hours. Contractual commitments during off-peak hours are generally met through purchases for resale. This sort of arrangement might actually increase the degree to which hourly water releases fluctuate, a situation that might contribute to downstream environmental and ecological impacts. In a series of simulations of the Glen Canyon facility, we demonstrate how the series of operating restrictions can mitigate some of the hourly fluctuations in water releases, thereby offsetting some of the downstream environmental and ecological impacts. Finally, using recreational benefit estimates from a previous study, we present a simple example that illustrates one trade-off, namely the trade-off between inexpensive hydroelectric power and downstream recreational benefits. We argue that policy-makers should weigh these and other trade-offs when deciding how to manage these facilities.

In the next two chapters we discuss hydraulically-coupled dams, so called because their operations are linked by a river that connects them. As we shall see, this will complicate questions of how these dams are to be managed.

NOTE

1. This chapter has evolved from Edwards, et al. (1999), 'Optimal provision of hydroelectric power under environmental constraints', *Land Economics*, **75** (2), 267–283.

8. Hydraulically-coupled dams: when one dam is not enough

Many dams in the world are connected to other dams by rivers. The existence of such hydraulically-coupled dams presents unique challenges to operators and resource managers. In previous chapters we have considered dams whose operations were self-contained. While water releases from one dam generated power and provided downstream uses of the water, we never considered the possibility that once the water was released it would be used for additional generation by another dam located downstream. Flows of water through the Columbia River, for example, are controlled by a series of 11 dams. Managing water flows through the Columbia River involves managing all 11 dams simultaneously. In Tasmania, the Derwent Catchment is made up of 16 dams, 10 power stations and a large number of smaller dams. For systems composed of multiple dams, the management problem becomes more complex. Releases from one dam provide water to downstream dams for additional generation and, because of head effects, not only influence the amount of water available for release by the downstream dam, but also influence the generating efficiency of these downstream dams. In this chapter we present a theoretical model of a system consisting of more than one dam. Following the lines of previous chapters, we will specify the production function and set up and solve the optimization problem for these hydraulically-coupled systems. In the next chapter, we present a case study of one such hydraulically-coupled system, the Aspinall Unit located in the state of Colorado, and present the results of simulations of this system to examine numerically many of the issues raised in this chapter.

8.1   A MODEL OF HYDRAULICALLY-COUPLED DAMS

Hydraulically-coupled dams have certainly been analysed before. Wood and Wollenberg (1996) present a basic model of such a system of dams. George et al. (1995) develop a model that examines short-term hydroelectric power scheduling for multiple dams along a river chain using integer programming methods. Yang and Read (1999) develop a model that optimises releases in a stochastic two-reservoir system in New Zealand. In contrast to these examples, the model presented here will follow closely those presented in previous chapters, will ignore the issue of uncertainty with respect to inflows and other variables, and will employ the same dynamic-programming methods seen in previous chapters.

Following the pattern established in previous chapters, we begin by specifying the production function for each of the dams in the system. For each of the dams, the production function is similar to those presented in previous sections, namely, generation depends on water release rates and reservoir content (our proxy for head), as given by:

$$q_t^j = q_t^j (r_t^j, W_t^j) \qquad (8.1)$$

In equation (8.1), q_t^j is hydroelectric generation from the jth facility in hour t, r_t^j is the rate of water release from the jth facility in period t and W_t^j is the content of the reservoir behind the jth facility in period t. What is different is that we have to first differentiate each dam and we do so by indexing each by $j = 1...,J$ for the J dams in the system.

The second and more substantive, difference is how the equations of motion for each dam are specified. These will differ from the equations of motion used in the previous models. For hydraulically-coupled facilities, each dam has its own equation of motion, but now the equations of motion will reflect the effects that water releases from upstream dams have on the content, elevation and head of downstream dams. For example, let us consider the middle dam in the Aspinall Unit, Morrow Point. Inflows into the Morrow Point reservoir will consist largely of water that has been released in previous periods from the upstream dam, which in this case is Blue Mesa. Releases from

Morrow Point will, in turn, be the principal source of inflows for the third dam in the Aspinall Unit, Crystal. These considerations lead us to modify our single-dam equation of motion to incorporate these linkages. The equation of motion for dam j is given by:

$$w_t^j = w_{t-1}^j - r_{t-1}^j + r_{t-1}^{j-1} \qquad (8.2)$$

For the jth dam, the reservoir content is depleted by releases from this dam, but supplemented by releases from the j-1th dam. In effect, we replace the inflow variable from previous chapters with releases from the upstream dam. Of course, for the topmost dam in a system, inflows are understood to occur in the same sense as occurred in previous chapters.

Having specified the production function and equation of motion, we can turn to the issue of revenues and costs. To maintain simplicity, we assume the same hydroelectric power dispatcher decides on how much water to release from each facility simultaneously. In effect, we assume the existence of a system manager that controls the three dams. We also assume that the power generated by the three dams is all sold in the same market. For example, we can think of the power being sold on a wholesale basis to a grid. For the time being, we also assume that the dam operator sells only the hydroelectric power generated and does not supplement sales with either thermal power generation or purchases for resale. When we turn to the simulations later on in this chapter, we will relax some of these assumptions.

Following previous chapters, we assume that the hydroelectric power dispatcher generates power and sells it in a large market, with the price given by the inverse demand function $p_t(Q_t)$ where Q_t represents the sum of electricity generated by the J dams and sold in period t. We can express industry output as $Q_t = \tilde{Q}_t + \sum_{j=1}^{J} q_t^j(r_t^j, W_t^j)$. $\tilde{Q}_t$ is defined as before as being the power sold by the other generators or energy marketers serving this particular market. Similarly, we assume that water release costs for the jth dam behave according to the cost function, $c_t^j(r_t^j)$, which we assume to be continuously differentiable with positive first- and second-derivatives. Finally, we are solving this problem in discrete time. This allows us to think of each time period as lasting one hour, which allows us to address hourly time-of-day variations in prices and other variables that might influence the dispatcher's decisions. Under this set of assumptions, profits in each period to the dispatcher are given by the following equation:

$$\pi_t = \sum_{j=1}^{J} p_t(Q_t) q_t^j(r_t^j, W_t^j) - c_t^j(r_t^j) \tag{8.3}$$

In the absence of any environmental restrictions, the only constraint that the dam operator faces is the equation of motion for each dam (given in equation 8.2).

The dispatcher will choose rates of water release to maximize the sum of net receipts subject to the equation of motion and the total water release constraint. The resulting Hamiltonian function is given by:

$$H = \sum_{j=1}^{J} [\sum_{t=1}^{T-1} \{p_t(Q_t) q_t^j(r_t^j, W_t^j) - c_t^j(r_t^j)$$
$$+ \gamma_{t+1}^j(W_{t+1}^j - W_t^j - r_t^j + r_t^{j-1})\}$$
$$+ p_T(Q_T) q_T^j(r_T^j, W_T^j) - c_T^j(r_T^j) \tag{8.4}$$
$$+ \gamma_T^j(W_T^j - r_T^j + r_T^{j-1})]$$

Following the conventions established in the previous chapter, we define γ_{t+1}^j as the discrete-time costate associated with the equation of motion for the jth water resource and define γ_T^j as the final period costate on the equation of motion for the jth water resource. The Kuhn–Tucker conditions on water releases for the jth dam in period t are given by:

$$\frac{\partial H}{\partial r_t^j} = p_t \frac{\partial q_t^j}{\partial r_t^j} + \frac{\partial p_t}{\partial q_t^j} \frac{\partial q_t^j}{\partial r_t^j} q_t^j - \frac{\partial c_t^j}{\partial r_t^j} - \gamma_{t+1}^j + \gamma_{t+1}^{j+1} \leq 0 \tag{8.5}$$

$$r_t \frac{\partial H}{\partial r_t} = 0 \qquad (8.6)$$

Assuming an interior solution, we can rearrange our Kuhn–Tucker first–order conditions to obtain the following relationship between the marginal benefits and marginal costs of releasing water for the jth dam:

$$p_t \frac{\partial q_t^j}{\partial r_t^j}(1 + \frac{1}{\eta_t}) = \frac{\partial c_t^j}{\partial r_t^j} + \gamma_{t+1}^j - \gamma_{t+1}^{j+1} \qquad (8.7)$$

As in previous chapters, the left-hand side of equation (8.7) represents the marginal benefit of releasing water from the jth facility. Similarly, the right-hand side of this equation is the marginal cost of releasing water from this facility. Notice, however, that this marginal cost term now includes the effects that releasing water from the jth dam has on the water resource shadow price for the downstream (j+1th) dam. Intuitively, releasing more water from the upstream dam makes additional water available for release through the downstream dam and, from the perspective of the operator managing the J dams simultaneously, reduces the marginal cost of releasing water from the jth facility.

8.2　ENVIRONMENTAL RESTRICTIONS AND HYDRAULICALLY-COUPLED DAMS

We now turn to the task of incorporating the same kinds of environmental restrictions that we considered in previous chapters. These restrictions will include minimum and maximum release constraints, ramping constraints and total water release requirements. These restrictions have been discussed in Chapters 6 and 7, so will not be repeated here. Moreover, the basic optimization problem will be analogous to that presented in Chapter 6. We assume that the operator will choose water release rates for the J dams to maximize the sum of discounted net receipts over the T periods. The objective function is given in equation (8.3) and the Hamiltonian for this problem is the following:

$$
\begin{aligned}
H = \sum_{j=1}^{J} [\sum_{t=1}^{T-1} \{ p_t(Q_t) q_t^j(r_t^j, W_t^j) - c_t^j(r_t^j) + \gamma_{t+1}^j(W_{t+1}^j - W_t^j - r_t^j + r_t^{j-1}) \\
- \delta_t^{uj}(r^{uj} - (r_t^j - r_{t-1}^j)) - \delta_t^{dj}(r^{dj} - (r_{t-1}^j - r_t^j)) \\
- \bar{\delta}_t^j(\bar{r}^j - r_t^j) + \tilde{\delta}_t^j(\tilde{r}^j - r_t^j) \} + \varphi_t^j(R^j - \sum_{t=1}^{T} r_t^j) \\
+ p_T(Q_T) q_T^j(r_T^j, W_T^j) - c_T^j(r_T^j) + \gamma_T^j(W_T^j - r_T^j + r_T^{j-1}) \\
- \delta_T^{uj}(r^{uj} - (r_T^j - r_{T-1}^j)) - \delta_T^{dj}(r^{dj} - (r_{T-1}^j - r_T^j)) \\
- \bar{\delta}_T^j(\bar{r}^j - r_T^j) + \tilde{\delta}_T^j(\tilde{r}^j - r_T^j)]
\end{aligned}
\tag{8.8}
$$

As in previous examples, we define γ_{t+1}^j as the discrete-time costate associated with the equation of motion for the jth water resource and define γ_T^j as the final period costate on the equation of motion for the jth water resource. We also define δ_t^{uj} as the discrete-time costate on the ramp-up constraint, δ_t^{dj} as the discrete-time costate on the ramp-down constraint, $\bar{\delta}_t^j$ as the discrete-time costate variable on the maximum release constraint and $\tilde{\delta}_t^j$ as the discrete-time costate on the minimum release constraint. Finally, we define φ_t^j as the discrete-time costate variable on the total water release requirement constraint. The final-period analogues to each of the costate variables are given by the final-period subscript.

In the absence of the environmental restrictions, the first-order conditions are similar to those presented above, but differ due to the inclusion of the total release constraint (which we assume to be binding in all of the examples we discuss). In the event of an interior solution, the first-order Kuhn–Tucker condition on water releases for the jth facility is given by:

$$p_t \frac{\partial q_t^j}{\partial r_t^j}(1+\frac{1}{\eta_t}) = \frac{\partial c_t^j}{\partial r_t^j} + \gamma_{t+1}^j - \gamma_{t+1}^{j+1} + \varphi_t^j \qquad (8.9)$$

Equation (8.9) can be given an interpretation analogous to previous models, that is, water will be released at a rate that equates the marginal benefits of releasing the water to the marginal costs of releasing the water, after incorporating the combined effects of the equations of motion for the jth and $j+1$th dams and the total water release requirement.

As before, the shadow price on the total water release constraint is amenable to multiple interpretations. A binding total water release constraint represents an upper bound on the amount of water that can be released which, if relaxed, induces more releases from the reservoir. On the other hand and since the constraint has to be satisfied with equality, it also represents a lower limit on the total amount of water to be released over the time horizon. This interpretation suggests that including the costate variable on the left-hand side of equation (8.9) might be appropriate, thereby encouraging the dispatcher to bring water release rates up to meet the constraint by the end of the time horizon.

In the event of an interior solution with a binding minimum release constraint, the first-order Kuhn–Tucker condition on water releases for the jth facility in period t implies the following:

$$p_t \frac{\partial q_t^j}{\partial r_t^j}(1+\frac{1}{\eta_t}) = \frac{\partial c_t^j}{\partial r_t^j} + \gamma_{t+1}^j - \gamma_{t+1}^{j+1} - \tilde{\delta}_t^j + \varphi_t^j \qquad (8.10)$$

This interpretation of equation (8.10) is essentially the same as the interpretation of equation (6.5). When this constraint is binding, additional water must be released to meet this constraint, thereby offsetting the potentially negative effects that the water resource and total water release constraints have on per-period water release rates.

In the event of an interior solution with a binding maximum release constraint, the first-order Kuhn–Tucker condition on water releases for the jth facility in period t implies the following:

$$p_t \frac{\partial q_t^j}{\partial r_t^j}(1 + \frac{1}{\eta_t}) = \frac{\partial c_t^j}{\partial r_t^j} + \gamma_{t+1}^j - \gamma_{t+1}^{j+1} + \bar{\delta}_t^j + \varphi_t^j \qquad (8.11)$$

In this case, water releases must be reduced to meet this constraint, thereby reinforcing the effects of the water resource constraint. Such could be the situation during periods of high demand when prices are higher, but expected to be lower in later periods of the time horizon. We can easily envision this occurring during on-peak hours of greater demand.

As we learned in Chapter 6, the effects of the minimum and maximum release constraints are felt directly in the periods in which water is released. The ramping restrictions, however, have impacts that extend beyond the own period. According to equation (8.12), the current period shadow price on the ramp-up constraint, δ_t^{uj}, discourages water releases in the current period. On the other hand, higher water releases in the current period also make meeting the ramp-up requirement in the next period easier. A binding next-period ramp-up requirement, as evidenced by its shadow price, δ_{t+1}^{uj}, being greater than zero, indicates that water releases can be increased in the current period to offset the effects of a binding ramp-up constraint in the current period:

$$p_t \frac{\partial q_t^j}{\partial r_t^j}(1 + \frac{1}{\eta_t}) = \frac{\partial c_t^j}{\partial r_t^j} + \gamma_{t+1}^j - \gamma_{t+1}^{j+1} - \delta_t^{uj} + \delta_{t+1}^{uj} \qquad (8.12)$$

In the event of an interior solution and binding ramp-down restriction, the first-order Kuhn–Tucker condition on water releases for the jth facility in period t implies the following:

$$p_t \frac{\partial q_t^j}{\partial r_t^j}(1 + \frac{1}{\eta_t}) = \frac{\partial c_t^j}{\partial r_t^j} + \gamma_{t+1}^j - \gamma_{t+1}^{j+1} + \delta_t^{dj} - \delta_{t+1}^{dj} \qquad (8.13)$$

As was the case in the model examined in Chapter 6, the current period shadow price on the ramp-down constraint, δ_t^{dj}, increases water releases in the current period. However, higher water releases in the current period also make meeting the ramp-down requirement in the next period more difficult. A binding next-period ramp-down requirement, as evidenced by its shadow price, δ_{t+1}^{dj}, being greater than zero, indicates that water releases can be reduced in the current period to offset the effects of a binding ramp-down constraint in the current period.

For hydraulically-coupled facilities, the total water release requirements play a very important role. A requirement that an upstream dam release a given quantity of water over a specific period, for example, one month, will ensure a fixed supply of water to the next dam in the chain. With a system consisting of a large number of dams, such water release requirements will require considerable coordination and planning on the part of the facility managers. Releasing too much water from an upstream dam could cause spillage in the downstream dam. Not releasing enough water from an upstream dam could reduce the amount of electricity generated by the downstream dam, but can also influence the amount of water that the downstream dam can release over the same period. In addition, the role that head effects play on generator efficiency means that the operator can use releases from one facility to influence the content of the downstream reservoir and thereby influence generator efficiency of the downstream dam to great advantage.

8.3   SUMMARY AND CONCLUSIONS

This chapter has presented the theoretical model of hydraulically-coupled dams. Following the lead in previous chapters, we first presented the theoretical model without environmental constraints and then introduced the environmental constraints to see how they affect dam operations. In many cases, dam operations do not change fundamentally with the linking of multiple dams. Operators will still load-follow and will respond to price incentives. However, the dam operator will account for the effects that decisions on one dam have on the operations of another dam, regardless of the presence of any operating restrictions. In particular, water releases from an upstream dam will influence the generating efficiency of the downstream dam.

In the next chapter, we present a case-study of one hydraulically-coupled system, namely the Aspinall Unit, which consists of three dams that operate on the Gunnison River in western Colorado. This case-study will be comprised of a simulation that links the three dams and includes the same kinds of operating restrictions that we have discussed in this and previous chapters.

9.   Hydraulically-coupled dams: a case study of the Aspinall Unit

In the previous chapter, we presented a theoretical model of a system composed of multiple dams connected by a common river. In this chapter, we present an application of one such system operating in the western United States, the Aspinall Unit, composed of three dams along the Gunnison River in western Colorado in the United States. We will apply the model developed in the first part of this chapter to the Aspinall Unit and present the results of simulations of this system.

9.1   THE ASPINALL UNIT

The unit consists of three dams, Blue Mesa, Morrow Point and Crystal located along the Gunnison River in western Colorado. These dams are operated by the Western Area Power Administration (United States Department of Energy). The model presented in this chapter has water cascading through the three dams which alters the generating efficiencies of each dam. As water flows through the three dams, changes in content cause changes in elevation, which in turn change the head of each dam. These changes in head change the generating efficiency of each facility. In order to operate the three facilities optimally, the model assumes that the dam operator will take these changes into account when determining hourly water release rates.

9.2   MODEL STRUCTURE

In the model of the Aspinall Unit, each dam will have an associated equation of motion. The content of the topmost dam in the chain, Blue

146

Mesa, is given by w_t^1, which depends on the content of that reservoir in the previous period, w_{t-1}^1, releases from Blue Mesa (r_{t-1}^1) in the previous period and inflows into Blue Mesa (f_{t-1}^1) in the previous period. Being the topmost dam in the chain, inflows into Blue Mesa are not the result of releases from any upstream dams included in our system. As a result, the equation of motion for Blue Mesa is given by $w_t^1 = w_{t-1}^1 - r_{t-1}^1 + f_{t-1}^1$, where we assign the index $j=1$ to Blue Mesa.

In contrast, inflows into the middle dam, Morrow Point, are releases from Blue Mesa. The equation of motion for Morrow Point is then $w_t^2 = w_{t-1}^2 - r_{t-1}^2 + r_{t-1}^1$, where we assign the index $j=2$ to Morrow Point. Inflows into the reservoir behind Morrow Point are represented by releases from Blue Mesa, or r_{t-1}^1. In analogous fashion, the equation of motion for Crystal is given by $w_t^3 = w_{t-1}^3 - r_{t-1}^3 + r_{t-1}^2$, where we assign the index $j=3$ to Crystal. Inflows into the reservoir behind Crystal are represented by releases from Morrow Point, or r_{t-1}^2. With these modifications to the equations of motion, we now have a system of three hydraulically-coupled dams.

The operator, who in previous chapters made decisions about one dam, with these decisions influencing the operating characteristics of that one dam, must now account for the effect the releases from one dam will have on the operating characteristics of the other dams. Not only will releasing water from one dam reduce the head of that dam, but it will also increase the head of the downstream dam. As in previous chapters, we assume that the operator decides on hourly rates of water release and purchases for resale in order to meet contractual commitments to customers at minimum cost. The operator is constrained by operational restrictions on maximum and minimum water releases and on elevation changes at Crystal. The simulations assume that elevation changes at Crystal are restricted to 10 feet over any 24-hour period and to 15 feet over any 72-hour period. Moreover, the operator is required to release fixed quantities of water from each dam during the period of simulation (one week).

The Aspinall Unit simulations are based on a version of the model that include separate equations for reservoir content, reservoir elevation and dam head, as was presented in Chapter 4. In this model, water releases (and inflows) change the content of the reservoir which changes the elevation of the reservoir. Changes in the elevation of the reservoir change the head of the dam. Changes in dam head change the efficiency of the generators. These effects are captured in the model and will be examined during our discussion of the simulation results.

Over the course of the simulation, water releases will change the content of each dam. The equations of motion for content of the reservoir are given in the equations discussed above. Changes in reservoir content will change the elevation of the dam through a linear equation of the form $E_t^j = \alpha_e^j + \beta_e^j W_t^j$, where the coefficients α_e^j and β_e^j have been estimated econometrically for each of the J facilities. Similarly, changes in elevation will change the dam head through a linear equation of the form $H_t^j = \alpha_h^j + \beta_h^j E_t^j$, where coefficients α_h^j and β_h^j have been estimated econometrically for each of the J facilities. Generation for each of the J facilities will be determined according to equations of the form $q_t^j = r_t^j H_t^j / \gamma^j$, where the coefficient γ^j has been determined econometrically. It turns out that this functional form for hydroelectric generation has a number of advantages when performing simulations. The first advantage is that it is relatively simple and one is required only to estimate one coefficient, namely, γ^j. Second, it reflects the combined roles that water releases and dam head have on generation. Third, the equation is non-linear and is thus more general than specific linear functional forms that, in reality, represent special cases of how hydroelectric power generation is specified. Fourth, models simulated using this form of the production function tend to solve easier than versions of the model using other functional forms (an important grass-roots consideration) and the models tend to be better behaved when this functional form is used. Some of these considerations are entirely subjective (and leave open the possibility of plenty of discussion) but are completely consistent with my own view that whenever possible, use simpler versions of equations rather than more complicated functional forms.

9.3   OPERATING RESTRICTIONS, DEMAND AND PRICES

In any case, the overall approach to the simulations presented in this chapter is similar to that of Chapter 7. The operator will choose rates of water release and purchases for resale to minimize the cost of meeting contractual power commitments to customers. The operator will be subject to constraints on the water resource (via the modified equations of motion for each facility as discussed above), constraints on total water releases from each facility over the course of the week, constraints on elevation changes at the Crystal facility and maximum release constraints on each facility. The maximum release constraints are based on generating capacity. Releases from Blue Mesa dam will be limited to a rate of 3700 CFS. Releases from Morrow Point will be limited to a rate of 4300 CFS and releases from Crystal will be limited to a rate of 1600 CFS. Changes in elevation at the Crystal facility will be limited to changing no more than 10 feet over a 24-hour period and 15 feet over a 72-hour period. Total releases from Blue Mesa will be limited to just over 24 000 acre-feet over the 168-hour period. Total releases from Morrow Point will be limited to just over 27 000 acre-feet over the 168-hour period. Total releases from Crystal will be limited to just under 29 000 acre-feet over the 168-hour period. In addition, bypass releases will be made at Crystal at a rate of 465 CFS over the 168-hour period. This will prevent the reservoir behind Crystal (a relatively small reservoir) from spilling.

The operator will charge customers a flat rate of $15 for each megawatt-hour of hydroelectric power generated and sold. Purchases for resale will be charged the wholesale spot price, plus an administrative charge of $2 per megawatt-hour. Wholesale spot prices will fluctuate with demand over the course of the week. Demand will range from just under 193 megawatt-hours to just under 356 megawatt-hours over the course of the week. Wholesale spot prices will range from just over $27 per megawatt-hour to $135.5 per megawatt-hour. The pattern of demand over the seven-day period is given in Figure 9.1. The slightly lower daily peaks that occur on the first and last days of the simulation occur because these days are a Sunday and Saturday (both days with lower peaks than would occur during the week). Wholesale spot prices will reflect a similar pattern, with slightly lower daily peaks on Sunday and Saturday.

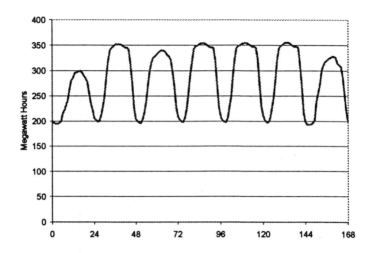

Figure 9.1 Demand

The pattern of wholesale spot prices is given in Figure 9.2.

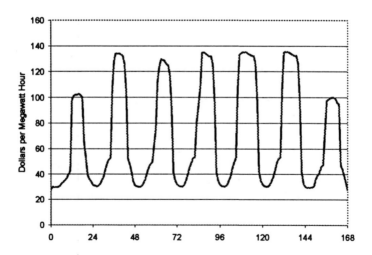

Figure 9.2 Wholesale spot prices

9.4   SIMULATION RESULTS

The results of the simulation indicate a pattern of water releases similar to that which occurred in the Chapter 7 simulations of the Power Marketing Administration, namely, the operator stores water during off-peak hours for release during on-peak hours. Off-peak demand not satisfied with hydroelectric power generation is met through purchases for resale. In this way, the operator meets the contractual commitment to its customers at minimum cost to their customers. Figure 9.3 illustrates the pattern of water release rates for each of the three dams.

Generation by the three facilities, along with purchases for resale, can be combined to show hourly power provision for the Aspinall Unit, as is done in Figure 9.4.

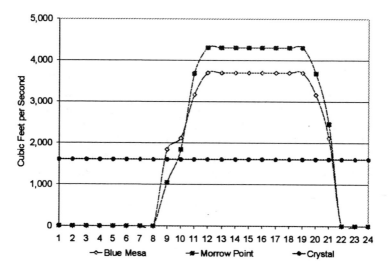

Figure 9.3 Hourly release rates: Aspinall Unit simulations

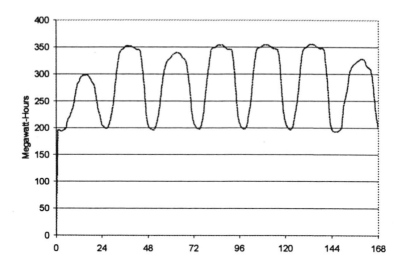

Figure 9.4 Hourly provision (generation plus purchases for resale)

Comparing Figure 9.4 to Figure 9.1 reveals how demand is met. We can create an additional series of figures that show what happens during each of the seven days of the week. These figures are based on averaging the first hour of each day and letting the result represent behaviour for the first hour of the representative day, averaging the second hour of each day and letting the result of that calculation represent behaviour for the second hour of the representative day and so on to create an average day. The following figure shows how hourly release rates vary over the course of the representative 24-hour period.

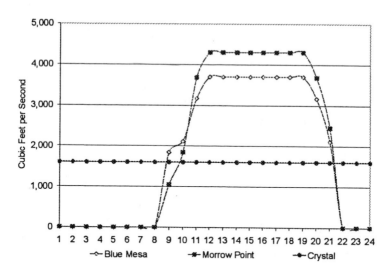

Figure 9.5 Hourly water release rates for representative 24-hour period

Figure 9.5 shows how the operator hydro-shifts each dam. The first eight hours of the representative day have no water being released from Blue Mesa or Morrow Point. For these dams over this period, water is stored in the reservoir and demand is satisfied through purchases for resale. As demand (and prices) increase over the next few hours, water is released from each of the dams to generate hydroelectric power. This pattern continues through the rest of the on-peak hours. As demand begins to drop off during the latter hours of the day, less water is released until the last two hours of the day when no water is released. Water is released at a constant rate from Crystal to satisfy the total water release requirement for that dam.

Figure 9.6 shows hydroelectricity generation from the three dams combined, purchases for resale and total power provision over the course of the representative 24-hour period. As is clear from this figure, off-peak demand is satisfied through purchase for resale (with the exception of Crystal) and on-peak demand is satisfied through hydroelectric power generation.

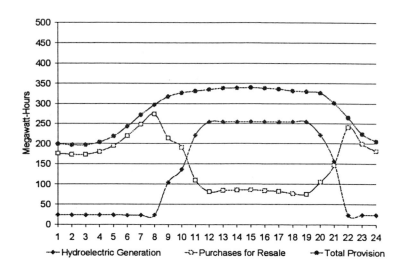

Figure 9.6 Hydroelectric generation, purchases for resale and total provision: representative 24-hour period

Throughout this book, we have emphasized the dual roles that the water resource plays in hydroelectric power generation. The simulation results presented thus far offer additional confirmation of the (obvious) result that releasing more water generates more hydroelectric power. We can also address the issue of how dam head affects the productivity of water releases by considering the results of the Aspinall Unit simulations presented in this chapter. In particular, we will focus on the Crystal dam, since this is the smallest of the dams and also because it experiences the largest (proportionate) change in content over the course of the week. This allows us to observe how the changes in content change elevation and dam head and hence generator efficiency.

As a result of the releases from Crystal and inflows from Morrow Point, the content, head and elevation of Crystal rise over the course of the week. Crystal's content starts out at 20 000 acre-feet and increases to just over 25 000 acre-feet by the end of the simulation. Crystal's elevation increases from 6740 to 6750 feet during the week, while

Crystal's dam head increases from just over 200 feet to just over 210 feet. The changes in head and content are illustrated in Figure 9.7.

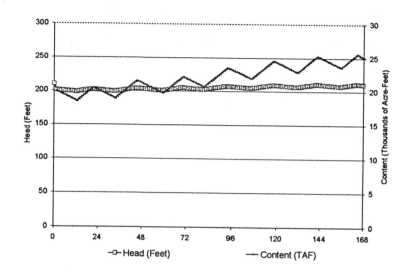

Figure 9.7 Dam head and content: Crystal

The increases in head should cause generating efficiency to increase over the course of the week. Over the course of the simulation, our simple definition of generator efficiency (generation divided by water release rate) increases from 14.5 to 15.18. Figure 9.8 compares how dam head and generator efficiency vary over the course of the simulation.

Since water releases from Crystal occur at a constant rate of 1600 CFS throughout the week, the saw-tooth pattern in Figure 9.8 is attributable to on-peak period releases from Morrow Point which cause the content of the Crystal reservoir to rise during on-peak hours. In effect, releasing water from Morrow Point has two benefits. First, water releases from Morrow Point generate hydroelectric power at Morrow Point. Second, water releases from Morrow Point increase the content and head at Crystal, thereby increasing generator efficiency at Crystal.

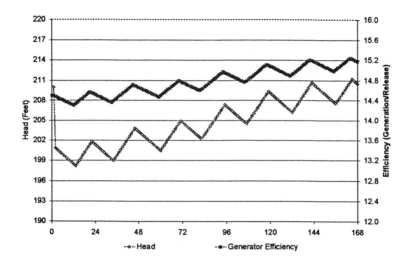

Figure 9.8 Dam head and generator efficiency: Crystal

9.5   CONTENT FLOWS SUMMARY

Another view of the above results is possible with what I will call a 'content-flows' summary, which shows how changes in net inflows change the content of each dam. We show such a summary for Blue Mesa in Figure 9.9. On the left vertical axis we measure net inflows, defined as inflows minus outflows (releases). The small hourly fluctuations that occur in net inflows are the result of our assumption that inflows fluctuate randomly over the course of the simulation. Nevertheless, inflows greater than zero mean that water is flowing into the reservoir faster than water is being released from the reservoir. During off-peak periods, inflows exceed releases, so the net inflows are positive. During on-peak periods, releases exceed inflows, so net inflows are negative.

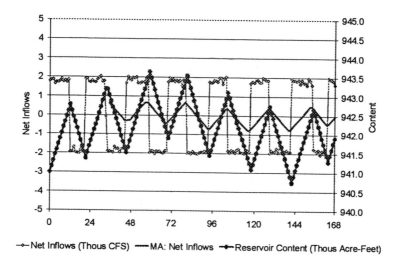

Figure 9.9 Content-flows summary: Blue Mesa dam

Hydro-shifting creates the alternating series of positive and negative inflows shown in the figure. On this axis, we also plot the 36-hour moving average of net inflows. This is plotted to smooth the net inflow series somewhat and, for this simulation, reveal a slight downward trend in net inflows. On the right vertical axis, we measure reservoir content. The up-and-down pattern exhibited by content is exaggerated by the selection of scale used, but illustrates how content changes from hour to hour. Over the course of the week, content tends to rise (as indicated by the rising peaks in content during the first few days), but eventually drops off as the simulation draws to a close (as indicated by the falling troughs in content during the last four days of the simulation). Figure 9.10 shows the content-flows summary for Morrow Point.

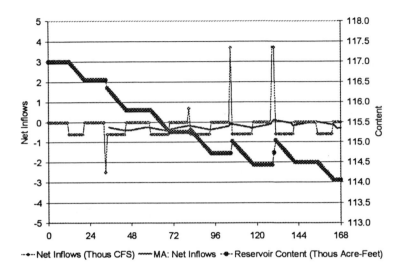

Figure 9.10 Content-flows summary: Morrow Point dam

For Morrow Point, net inflows fluctuate between zero during off-peak periods and negative during on-peak periods. Evidently, off-peak period releases from Blue Mesa (which provide inflows into Morrow Point) are exactly offset by off-peak period releases from Morrow Point. As a result, the moving average of net inflows hovers below zero throughout most of the week. The periodic spikes in net inflows that occur later in the week bring the moving average of net inflows closer to zero (and slightly positive in some cases). However, the overall trend in net inflows is negative, which explains the reduction in content that occurs over the course of the week. Figure 9.11 shows the content-flows summary for Crystal.

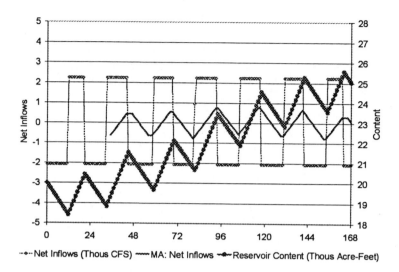

Figure 9.11 Content-flows summary: Crystal dam

In contrast to the Blue Mesa and Morrow Point dams, the content of Crystal rises over the course of the simulation. While net inflows fluctuate throughout the week, the on-peak inflows (i.e., on-peak releases from Morrow Point) exceed the constant releases from Crystal. This causes content to increase over the course of the week.

9.6   SUMMARY AND CONCLUSIONS

This chapter illustrates the application of the model developed in Chapter 8 to an actual hydraulically-coupled system of dams. Of principal interest is how release rates vary by time of day and how generating efficiencies vary with reservoir content and dam head. Moreover, the simulations in this chapter illustrate how a dam operator will account for these factors in deciding when to release water. The task of extending this model to systems containing more than three dams should not be too difficult. As with all simulation models, complications arise in the specification and calibration phases of developing these models. The problem of specifying the model involves ensuring that the different pieces of the model fit together well. For example, one must ensure that the equations of motion that link the dams are specified correctly so that releases from one dam will result in inflows to the downstream dam. Moreover, the equations for elevation and head must be specified to yield empirically sensible results, namely, that their values will change by the right magnitudes when the reservoir content changes.

There are still many issues that we have not addressed. For one, we have not attempted to link changes in release rates to specific downstream environmental or ecological impacts. While many of the operating restrictions imposed on the three dams that make up the Aspinall Unit (as well as the other dams considered in previous chapters) are designed to mitigate any potentially negative environmental and ecological impacts, we have not attempted to integrate these considerations into the model explicitly. Such an explicit treatment of these impacts would require that we take a very close look at how releases and changes in release rates affect the downstream environment. Taking such a look in any analytical sense would require that we specify some damage function that maps releases (and changes in release rates) to changes in the downstream environment.

In addition, we have made no attempt to integrate this model into a broader market setting. Such a view would allow us to consider the impacts of wholesale electricity market deregulation on how dam operators behave. One of the results of the model presented in this chapter and in Chapter 7 was that water release rates fluctuated with wholesale spot prices. Whether or not we can argue that deregulation has resulted in more volatility in wholesale prices and whether this increased volatility has changed the volatility of hourly water release rates, cannot be established in the analysis conducted thus and represents one possible topic for future research.

10. Summary and conclusions

The preceding chapters have presented a brief introduction to the economics of dams and hydroelectric power. While most of the issues raised in the introduction to this book remain unanswered, I hope that this book has laid some foundation for subsequent analyses and resolution of at least some of these issues. The series of models presented in later chapters, while simple, couch the entire discussion of hydroelectric power firmly in the natural resource economics domain, and more specifically, in the water management domain. This treatment reflects my own view, as pointed out in the introduction, that ultimately we are making decisions on how to manage water resources and one such use of this water resource is hydroelectric power generation.

After a brief historical introduction to dams and water use, we discussed the regulation of hydroelectric power, with an emphasis on recent United States history. How dams are regulated and how the hydroelectric power generated by these dams is priced, will likely be subjects of considerable debate in the future. Some have suggested that many of these dams should be decommissioned, some have argued that hydroelectric power should be privatized, and others have argued that even without privatization, the hydroelectric power should at least be sold to utilities and other customers at spot market rates, rather than based on the current system-wide average cost recovery basis currently in use. While I tend to be quite sympathetic towards the last of these propositions, I cannot say that any of the analysis presented in this book brings us any closer to resolving these and many of the other issues. Users of hydroelectric power are no different than users of any other resource, good or service. Low prices encourage consumption.

Chapter 7 presented a case-study of a dam operated by one of the US Power Marketing Administrations (PMA). One of the implications of this chapter is that the manner in which the hydroelectric power is priced, and given the objective of the PMA to satisfy these contract commitments to their customers at minimum cost, might not be the most socially desirable way of marketing hydroelectric power. Lower on-peak prices encourage generation during on-peak periods, making what is ordinarily a relatively cheaper source of electricity a source of power that is primarily used during on-peak periods. Anyone desirous of a system of rules that encourages energy conservation would be hard-pressed to rationalize a pricing system that actually encourages use during that part of the day when demand is highest. Moreover, the manner in which the hydroelectric power is priced might also have implications for the health of the downstream environment. The intent of the operating restrictions discussed in this and other chapters is to mitigate some, if not all, of the fluctuating flows and many of the simulations illustrated that these operating restrictions indeed reduce the extent of these fluctuations. On the other hand, regulatory reforms that changed the way in which the hydroelectric power is priced would generate their own set of regional economic impacts. To the extent that customers pay higher prices for hydroelectric power, particularly during on-peak times, end-users would likely pay higher rates for electricity. From a social welfare point of view, we face a trade-off between cheap hydroelectric power and fluctuating downstream flows.

After our brief overview of natural resource economics and our discussion explaining the rudiments of hydroelectric power generation, we presented our first model of a hydroelectricity generating facility and illustrated the dual roles that water plays in hydroelectric generation, namely the flow and stock (for lack of better terms) values of the water. Herein lies one of the rationales for the dynamic modelling, as well as the more general non-linear approach to modelling hydroelectric power generation taken in this book, namely, that releasing water now has implications for future generation that might be less transparent if we confined our view to a static model and linear generating technology. We then introduced the joint provision of hydroelectric power and thermally-generated power, a common occurrence for many hydroelectric facilities in the United States and surely no less common in other countries. We finally introduced the notion of operating restrictions in Chapter 6 and this served as a foundation for the models presented in Chapters 7 to 9.

Following the pattern established in Chapters 6 and 7, Chapters 8 and 9 presented an analysis of hydraulically-coupled systems, first with a theoretical model and then with a case-study of the Aspinall Unit in

Colorado. The model presented in these chapters can, of course, be extended to any arbitrary number of dams, so what we have learned from that model can be applied to other systems and can be extended to address other issues relating to multiple dam systems. We did not cover pumped storage, the practice of pumping water from the afterbay of a dam into the forebay for release, usually during on-peak times when the hydroelectric power is more valuable. This is one topic eligible for treatment in future research.

We have also made no attempt to integrate the dams modelled in these chapters into larger electricity generation, transmission and distribution systems, nor have we addressed issues of public policies towards the energy industry in general. Of course, by this I refer to recent deregulation of bulk power markets in the United States. On the other hand, local electricity markets are in the process of being deregulated (Salpukas, 1998). It will be interesting to see what implications this might have for hydroelectric power.

Last, but not least, we have not attempted in any systematic way to develop environmental damage (or benefit) functions that tie water release rates, or variations in water release rates, to specific environmental or ecological impacts. Given the breadth of possible downstream impacts, such an undertaking might best occur on a case-by-case basis. For example, fluctuations in water release can cause impacts on the distribution of sediment downstream, it can cause changes in the make-up of vegetation downstream and it can cause the ecology of downstream rivers to change. Modelling changes in sediment alone would be a likely candidate for another book-length treatment. Moreover, attempting to assign monetary values to any of these changes (in the honourable and valiant attempt to conduct something closely approaching cost–benefit analysis), might generate just as much controversy as any issues it attempts to resolve. This is not to suggest that such attempts should not be made. On the contrary, proper evaluation of policy towards dams and hydroelectric power should proceed in a structured and systematic manner and should attempt to integrate pricing rules and regulatory schemes with water release patterns and their resulting environmental, ecological and recreational impacts. The development and use of adaptive management is certainly one step in this direction.

Bibliography

Anderson, L.G. (1986), *The Economics of Fisheries Management*, Baltimore, MD and London: Johns Hopkins University Press.

Arrow, K.J. and S. Chang (1982), 'Optimal pricing, use, and exploration of uncertain natural resource stocks', *Journal of Environmental Economics and Management* (9), 1–10.

Arrow, K.J. and M. Kurz (1970), *Public Investment, The Rate of Return, and Optimal Fiscal Policy*, Baltimore, MD and London: Johns Hopkins University Press for Resources for the Future.

Axelrod, R. (1985), *The Evolution of Cooperation*, Basic Books.

Axelrod, R. (ed.) (1997), *The Complexity of Cooperation: Agent-Based Models of Competition and Collaboration*, Princeton, NJ: Princeton University Press.

Batstone, S.R.J. and T.J. Scott (1998), 'Long-term contracting in a deregulated electricity industry: simulation results from a hydro management model', *Proceedings of the ORSNZ 33 Annual Conference*, 147-56.

Beverton, R.J.H. and S.J. Holt (1957), *On the Dynamics of Exploited Fish Populations*, London: Ministry of Agriculture, Fisheries and Food Fisheries Investigation Series, 2 (19).

Bishop, R.C., K.J. Boyle, M.P. Welsh and R.M. Baumgartner (1987), *Glen Canyon Releases and Downstream Recreation: An Analysis of User Preferences and Economic Values*, Final Report to the Recreation Subteam of the Glen Canyon Environmental Studies, Flagstaff, AZ: US Bureau of Reclamation.

Brooke, A., D. Kendrick, A. Meeraus and R. Raman (1998), *GAMS: A User's Guide*, Washington, DC: GAMS Development Corporation.

Brown, G.B., Jr. (1974), 'An optimal program for managing common property resources with congestion externalities', *Journal of Political Economy* (82), 163–174.

Brown, S.J. and D.S. Sibley (1986), *The Theory of Public Utility Pricing*, Cambridge: Cambridge University Press.

Burt, O.R. (1964), 'Optimal resource use over time with an application to groundwater', *Management Science* (11), 80–93.

Burt, O.R. and R.G. Cummings (1970), 'Production and investment in natural resource industries', *American Economic Review* (60), 576–90.

Bushnell, J. (1998), 'Water and power: hydroelectric resources in the era of competition in the western US', Berkeley: University of California Energy Institute, PWP-056.

Carlson, J.L. and S.C. Palmer (1997), 'Effects of a change in streamflows on recreation use values: an application of benefits transfer', *Rivers*, 6 (1), 32–43.

Chiang, A. (1992), *Elements of Dynamic Optimization*, Prospect Heights, IL: Waveland Press.

Christy, F.T., Jr. and A.D. Scott (1965), *The Common Wealth in Ocean Fisheries*, Baltimore, MD: Johns Hopkins University Press.

Clark, C.W. (1976), *Mathematical Bioeconomics: The Optimal Management of Renewable Resources*, New York: John Wiley & Sons.

Collier, M.P., R.W. Webb and E.D. Andrews (1997), 'Experimental flooding in Grand Canyon', *Scientific American*, 82–89.

Conrad, J.M. (1999), *Resource Economics*, Cambridge: Cambridge University Press.

Conrad, J.M. and C.W. Clark (1987), *Natural Resource Economics: Notes and Problems*, New York: Cambridge University Press.

Crew, M.A. and P.R. Kleindorfer (1978), 'Reliability and public utility pricing', *American Economic Review*, 68 (1), 31–40.

Crutchfield, J.A. and A. Zellner (1962), 'Economic aspects of the Pacific halibut fishery', *Fishery Industrial Research*, 1 (1), Washington, DC: US Department of the Interior.

Dasgupta, P.S. and G.M. Heal (1979), *Economic Theory and Exhaustible Resources*, Cambridge: James Nisbet & Co. and Cambridge University Press.

Deacon, R.T. (1985), 'The simple analytics of forest economics', in Deacon, R.T. and M.B. Johnson (eds), *Forestlands Public and Private*, San Francisco, CA: Balinger.

Disheroon, F.R. (1993), 'Hydroelectric power', in Campbell-Mohn, C., B. and J. William Futrell (eds), *Environmental Law: From Resources to Recovery*, St Paul, MN: West Publishing Company.

The Economist (1997), 'The dammed', 30 October.

The Economist (2000a), 'Kenyan gloom', 29 June.

The Economist (2000b), 'Rural unrest', 6 July.

The Economist (2000c), 'A good year for alewives', 27 July.

The Economist (2001), 'Beyond the pool', 1 March.

Edwards, B.K., S.J. Flaim and J.D. Ancrile (1992), 'Maximizing the value of thermally integrated hydroelectric generating facilities', in Vogt, W.G. and M.H. Mickle (eds), *Modeling and Simulation, Proceedings of the Twenty-Third Annual Pittsburgh Conference on Modeling and Simulation*, 463–70.

Edwards, B.K., R.E. Howitt and S.J. Flaim (1996), 'Fuel, crop, and water substitution in irrigated agriculture', *Resource and Energy Economics*, 18 (3), 311–31.

Edwards, B.K., S.J. Flaim and R.E. Howitt (1999), 'Optimal provision of hydroelectric power under environmental constraints', *Land Economics*, 75 (2), 267–83.

Ferguson, C.E. (1972), *Microeconomic Theory*, Homewood, IL: Richard D. Irwin, Inc.

Fisher, A.C. (1981), *Resource and Environmental Economics*, Cambridge: Cambridge University Press.

Fisher, A.C., W.M. Hanemann and A.G. Keeler (1991), 'Integrating fishery and water resource management: a biological model of a California salmon fishery', *Journal of Environmental Economics and Management*, 20, 234–61.

Francfort, J. (1997), 'Hydropower's contribution to carbon dioxide emission reduction', Idaho National Engineering and Environmental Laboratory, November.

French, H.W. (1998), 'A drought halts Ghana on its road to success', *New York Times*, 15 March.

Georgakakos, A.P., H. Yao and Y. Yu (1997a), 'A control model for dependable hydropower capacity optimization, *Water Resources Research*, 33 (10), 2349–65.

Georgakakos, A.P., H. Yao and Y. Yu (1997b), 'Control models for hydroelectric energy optimization', *Water Resources Research*, 33 (10), 2367–79.

George, J.A., E.G. Read, R.E. Rosenthal and A.L. Kerr (1995), 'Optimal scheduling of hydro stations: an integer programming model', EMRG Working Paper EMRG-WP-95-07, Department of Management, University of Canterbury, New Zealand.

Gordon, H.S. (1954), 'The economic theory of a common property resource: the fishery', *Journal of Political Economy* 62, 124–42.

Hadley, G. (1964), *Nonlinear and Dynamic Programming*, Reading, MA: Addison-Wesley.

Hamlen, W. and J. Tschirhart (1980), 'Solar energy, public utilities, and economic efficiency', *Southern Economic Journal*, 47 (2), 348–65.

Hanser, P., J. Wharton and P. Fox-Penner (1997), 'Real-time pricing–restructuring's big bang?', *Public Utilities Fortnightly*, 135 (5).

Harden, B. (2001), 'River's power aids California and enriches the northwest', *The New York Times*, 1 May.

Hartman, R. (1976), 'The harvesting decision when a standing forest has value', *Economic Inquiry*, 14, 52–58.

Hodge, T. (2001), 'Optimal provision of hydroelectric and other water use benefits under environmental constraints', unpublished paper, Colorado School of Mines.

Hotelling, H. (1931), 'The economics of exhaustible resources', *Journal of Political Economy*, 39, 137–75.

Howe, C.W. (1979), *Natural Resource Economics: Issues, Analysis, and Policy*, New York: John Wiley & Sons.

International Commission on Large Dams (1998), *World Register of Dams, 1998*.

Jackson, R. (1973), 'Peak load pricing model of an electric utility using pumped storage', *Water Resources Research*, 9 (3), 556–562.

Johansson, P.-O. and K.-G. Löfgren (1985), *The Economics of Forestry and Natural Resources*, Oxford: Basil Blackwell.

Lane, M. (1973), 'Conditional chance constrained model for reservoir control', *Water Resources Research*, 9 (4), 937–48.

Levhari, D., R. Michener and L.J. Mirman (1981), 'Dynamic programming models of fishing: competition', *American Economic Review*, 71 (4), 649–61.

Liu, Pan-Tai (ed.) (1980), *Dynamic Optimization and Mathematical Economics*, New York: Plenum Press.

Mirman, L.J. and D.F. Spulber (eds) (1982), *Essays in the Economics of Renewable Resources*, Amsterdam: North-Holland Publishing Company.

Panzar, J.C. and D.S. Sibley (1978), 'Public utility pricing under risk: the case of self-rationing', *American Economic Review*, 888–95.

Phillips, C.F. (1988), *The Regulation of Public Utilities: Theory and Practice*, Public Utilities Reports.

Pindyck, R.A. (1978), 'The optimal exploration and production of nonrenewable resources', *Journal of Political Economy*, 86, 841–61.

Pindyck, R.A. (1980), 'Uncertainty and natural resource markets', *Journal of Political Economy*, 88, 1203–25.

Plourde, C.G. (1970), 'A simple model of replenishable natural resource exploitation', *American Economic Review*, 60, 518–22.

Pontryagin, L.S., V.S. Boltyanskii, R.V. Gamrelidze and E.F. Mischenko (1962), *The Mathematical Theory of Optimal Processes*, New York: Wiley-Interscience.

Reisner, M. (1993), *Cadillac Desert: The American West and Its Disappearing Water*, New York: Penguin.

Reuters (2001), 'Brazil may face rolling blackouts', 31 May.

Reznicek, K.K. and S.P. Simonovic (1990), 'An improved algorithm for hydropower optimization', *Water Resources Research*, 26 (2), 189–98.

Rosig, J. and G.C. Garza (1967), 'Benefits obtained from the optimal operation of hydroelectric power systems', Stanford University: Department of Engineering-Economics.

Saad, M., P. Bigras, A. Turgeon and R. Durquette (1996), 'Fuzzy learning decomposition for the scheduling of hydroelectric power systems', *Water Resources Research*, 32 (1), 179–86.

Salpukas, A. (1998), 'Revenue streams from an old source', *The New York Times*, 29 November.

Samuelson, P.A. (1976), 'Economics of forestry in an evolving society', *Economic Inquiry*, 14, 466–92.

Scott, A.D. (1955), 'The fishery: the objective of sole ownership', *Journal of Political Economy*, 63, 116–24.

Silberberg, E. (1990), *The Structure of Economics: A Mathematical Analysis*, New York: McGraw-Hill.

Smith, V.L. (1968), 'Economics of production from natural resources', *American Economic Review*, 58, 409–31.

Steiner, P.O. (1957), 'Peak loads and efficient pricing', *Quarterly Journal of Economics*, 585–610.

Stiglitz, J.E. (1976), 'Monopoly and the rate of extraction of exhaustible resources', *American Economic Review*, 71 (4), 655–61.

Takayama, A. (1984), *Mathematical Economics*, Cambridge: Cambridge University Press.

Thomas, G., A. Winston and G. Wright (1972), 'New approach to water allocation under uncertainty', *Water Resources Research*, 8 (5), 1151–58.

Turvey, R. (1964), 'Optimization and suboptimization in fishery regulation', *American Economic Review*, 54, 64–76.

United States Department of the Interior, Bureau of Reclamation (1991), *Hydropower 2002 Reclamation's Energy Initiative.*

United States Department of the Interior, Bureau of Reclamation (1996), *Power Program Fact Sheet.*

United States Department of the Interior, Bureau of Reclamation (1998), *Reclamation's Role in Hydropower, Overview of the Electric Utility Industry,* available at http://www.usbr.gov/power/data/ role_rpt.htm.

United States Department of the Interior, Bureau of Reclamation (2001a), *Hydroelectric Power,* Bureau of Reclamation Power Resources Office.

United States Department of the Interior, Bureau of Reclamation (2001b), *The History of Hydropower Development in the United States,* Revised, 16 August 2001, available at http://www.usbr.gov /power/edu/history.htm.

United States General Accounting Office (1996), *Power marketing administration, cost recovery, financing and comparison to nonfederal utilities,* GAO/AIMD-96-145.

United States General Accounting Office (1997), *Federal power: issues related to the divestiture of federal hydropower resources,* GAO/RCED-97-48.

Varian, H.R. (1992), *Microeconomic Analysis,* New York: W.W. Norton & Company.

Verhovek, S.H. (2000), 'Power shortage sends ripples across west', *New York Times,* 17 December.

Wall Street Journal, 15 August 1996, page C15.

Walters, C.J. (1986), *Adaptive Management of Renewable Resources,* New York: McMillan.

Western Area Power Administration (1991a), *Annual Report* (and Statistical Appendix).

Western Area Power Administration (1991b), *Power Marketing Alternatives,* Western Area Power Administration, Salt Lake City Area Integrated Projects.

Wood, A.J. and B.F. Wollenberg (1996), *Power Generation, Operation, and Control,* New York: John Wiley & Sons.

World Commission on Dams (2000), *Dams and Development: A New Framework for Decision-Making,* London and Sterling, VA: Earthscan Publications.

Yang, M. and E.G. Read (1999), 'A constructive dual dp for a reservoir model with correlation', EMRG Working Paper EMRG-

WP-99-01, Department of Management, University of Canterbury, New Zealand.

Index

Y

Z